HIGH

PERFORMING

COACH

HIGH
PERFORMING
COACH

THE FIVE ESSENTIAL ELEMENTS OF BUILDING A HIGH-FEE COACHING BUSINESS ONLINE & FROM THE HEART

RYAN MATHIE

Published by Best Seller Publishing®, St. Augustine, FL
Best Seller Publishing® is a registered trademark.
Printed in the United States of America.

ISBN:978-1-962595-37-7

This publication is designed to provide accurate and authoritative information with regard to the subject matter covered. It is sold with the understanding that the publisher is not engaged in rendering legal, accounting, or other professional advice. If legal advice or other expert assistance is required, the services of a competent professional should be sought. The opinions expressed by the author in this book are not endorsed by Best Seller Publishing® and are the sole responsibility of the author rendering the opinion.

For more information, please write:
Best Seller Publishing®
53 Marine Street
St. Augustine, FL 32084
or call 1 (626) 765-9750
Visit us online at: www.BestSellerPublishing.org

Contents

Dear Reader,

As I embark on the exciting journey of sharing the insights and experiences within these pages, I want to offer a brief context to our shared exploration. The words you are about to read were penned during my tenure as the CEO of High-Performing Coaching which I originally co founded in 2019. Life, however, is an ever-evolving journey, and since then, my path has taken a different turn. I've stepped away from my role as CEO as of the end 2023, but the essence of the lessons and stories captured in this book remains timeless. While the context of my current position may have changed, the wisdom and inspiration within these pages are as relevant as ever. I invite you to join me in this exploration, embracing the evolution of both author and reader as we navigate the transformative landscape of the written word.

Let's begin.

Acknowledgements

First and foremost, I want to acknowledge the entire team at HPC (especially Adrian Shiel) for all your dedication, commitment, and absolute stand for our clients.

To our clients, the real heroes. Thank you for believing in us as we have believed in you, and mostly, thank you for believing in yourself.

To Best Seller Publishing (especially Rob Kosberg, Bob Harpole, Matt Schnarr, Kathleen Shewman, Elizabeth Slocum, Meghan McDonald, and Elizabeth Huston) for all the brilliant support in helping me write this book!

To Daniel Priestley for writing the foreword to this book and for his support over the years. To all my mentors, coaches, teachers, trainers, and guides, some of whom are mentioned in this book and others — you know who you are. Thanks for all it took on your part to get yourself to the point where you were able to make such a contribution to me.

And finally, to you. Thank you for picking up and reading this book and letting me into your world so that I may have the opportunity to contribute to you and your journey. I don't take it for granted, and I trust that it will serve you in a meaningful way.

To all of you and more, from the bottom of my heart, thank you.

Two Artists

Two artists talking ...

Inspired and energised through the power of a commitment ...

Clearing away the old, making space for someone new.

Vibrant colours of distinct applications call forth secret dreams and breathtaking views.

A process of creation and a new vision declared. A choice to believe that which must be chosen and believed, moment by moment, over and over again.

Courage, freedom, trust, love ... a life fulfilled is my body of work.

Two artists just sitting and talking ...
One of the artists is me ...
And the other artist is you.

— Ryan Mathie

This book is dedicated to you, the one and only true creator of your life.

Foreword

There are conversations that change everything. They could be short and sharp, but they have the impact of changing the direction of your life. Sometimes a powerful conversation evolves over a year. It might meander across a set of problems, or it might create unresolved tension and then inspire gradual actions that never would have happened but for the conversation.

It strikes me as incredible that conversations happen nonstop, every waking moment of our lives. We have conversations constantly with our friends, partners, business associates, and clients. Even when we are alone, we start having conversations with ourselves. With so much conversation happening, it's surprising to think how few conversations are meaningful.

It is a rare gem to experience a moment when someone's words hit you like a rugby tackle. We need these rare conversations to make our lives work. Without the right conversations, you wouldn't have the most valuable aspects of your life. You don't get married without a few great conversations. You don't start businesses without powerful conversations.

Without powerful conversations, you don't get a team of people working together, you don't get investors trusting you. You don't get the house, the car, the holidays, or the lucky breaks you want without first having the conversations that lead to these things.

What separates humans from the animal kingdom? Largely, it's the conversations we have.

You've already been on the receiving end of a powerful conversation. At some point in your life, someone changed your mind about something; they got you to do something you otherwise wouldn't have done by verbally dragging you out of your comfort zone. I'm sure you've seen someone give a powerful speech that magnetised your attention and shifted your perspective. Of course you have spoken to a sales professional who has artfully raised your excitement levels and guided you to act. You've made commitments, you've taken actions, and you've moved your focus as a result of conversations other people have had with you.

Now it's time for you to be the source of more powerful conversations more often — which is what this book is going to help you do.

What if you could choose to have more powerful conversations every day? What if you knew the right way to discuss your value? What if you could powerfully talk about money? What if you could get paid huge amounts of money because of the way you conducted a conversation? The truth is, this is the ONLY way you'll earn huge amounts of money and have the life you desire. At some level, everything you want is on the other side of powerful conversations.

Coaches get paid because they become masters at having powerful conversations that change people's lives for the better. The world's highest-paid coaches know when to bring silence into a conversation, when to ask a question that shifts someone's perception, how to reflect back to people a synthesis of what they were thinking, and how to introduce some radical new ideas.

Whether it's making a sale or delivering remarkable value, High-Performing Coaches are high-performing conversationalists.

This book is going to take you into the art of having powerful conversations. Ryan is going to show you how to enrol clients, how to conduct great coaching sessions, and how to inspire your coaching clients to say things that change their lives for the better.

Ryan is an award-winning, globally renowned masterful trainer and coach. He has a winning combination of passion, intelligence, empathy, humour, and depth. He has the charismatic spark that draws you in and holds your attention — but there's more to it than a natural gift. Ryan has studied powerful conversations deeply and from multiple angles. He knows how to enrol people as enthusiastic clients with an ethical stance and inspiring ease. He knows how to get his clients to transform with hard-hitting, elegant, and focused coaching. He knows how to get people to take a positive step forward — his words lead people to actions, and those people go on to create astonishing results.

When it comes to having powerful coaching and enrolment conversations, some people know the theory, and some people know how to do it themselves; very few people know how to transfer this rare and valuable skill to others. Ryan is going to share cornerstone skills that will make you a more valued communicator.

As you read this book, you are going to gain the skills, the confidence, and the insights required to make you a high-performing conversationalist and a High-Performing Coach.

— Daniel Priestley,
author of the bestselling
books *Key Person of Influence,*
Entrepreneur Revolution,
Oversubscribed, and *24 Assets*

Introduction

I am excited and grateful that you've chosen to read this book and made the decision to become a High-Performing Coach.

When I refer to a 'coach', I am really speaking of all purpose-driven entrepreneurs, dedicating their lives to their own personal transformation, who are open, willing, and ready to break through whatever is standing in their way and contribute all they've learned to those who are open and willing to receive.

You may refer to yourself as an author, speaker, therapist, healer, doctor, and so on, but for the purposes of this book I will refer to you as 'coach'.

This book is dedicated to you.

To remind you of who you are.

What you are capable of.

The impact you can make.

And to open you up to limitless possibilities in your coaching business and in your life.

Creating the remarkable results you want for yourself and your clients hinges on two basic principles.

First, what is going on inside of you: your views, opinions, and beliefs. These are your thoughts. To say it another way, it's the conversation that you are generating for yourself: what you say to yourself and what you speak out into the world to others.

You'll learn in this book that it's all just a conversation, and the conversation you are having creates your world.

Second, what is going on outside of you: the actions you are taking or not taking. This is your strategy. To say it another way, it's what you are doing and what you are not doing.

It is this potent combination of high-vibrational and deliberate thinking and speaking combined with tried, tested, and effective action that creates phenomenal results.

This book shows you how to do both so that you can access the startling truth: that building a profitable, high-fee, online coaching business can be done from the heart and with velocity.

We will dive deeply and precisely into the skill of thinking thoughts and generating conversations with yourself and others that are aligned with who you truly are and what you want to create. I call this 'Unshakeable Belief'.

I'm also going to show you the most effective strategies to launch your business and create high-paying clients, one powerful conversation at a time.

My intention is for this book to become a road map for your own personal and professional journey towards astonishing growth and true success (which also, and most certainly, includes the flow of money to you).

My commitment to you is that, as you apply the ideas, you will have a transformation both inside yourself and out there in your business.

You will experience a radical shift in who you are, how you relate to yourself, how you think, how you speak, and how you show up for your clients, so you can help them break through as you have broken through.

To that end, this book is as much about you and me working in collaboration as it is about my coaching you. Together, we can make an exponential impact, and for that, I am truly grateful. Thank you in advance for your partnership; I don't take it lightly, and it leaves me feeling touched, grateful, and inspired.

Since 2011, I have stood on hundreds of stages and worked with thousands of people all over the world. In HPC alone, I've personally enrolled over $2 million worth of high-fee clients. In a single day, I've enrolled 30+ high-paying clients from a stage, generating over $150,000 in revenue.

I have directly coached thousands of coaches, and thousands more indirectly, to create millions of dollars in their business — a huge amount of revenue that almost feels like a fairy tale, except it's real. I have mentored coaches in all niches (with no experience all the way through to 20+ years of experience) and watched them create breakthrough results in their coaching businesses — for themselves and their clients.

The dollar value here, however, is exciting on one hand and relatively irrelevant on the other.

Money without fulfilment was never a big enough game for me; I'm a hippie at heart.

And I know money alone isn't a big enough game for you either, which (like me) is why you chose to be a Coach.

Money, like everything else that may be wanted, is deserved and available in abundance, and the amount you have versus how much you want is simply an indicator of something much more important: it's a measure of your personal growth and your significant impact on the lives of others. The value of one life changed, let alone thousands, is literally priceless to me.

My personal results were not achieved without effort or support. I've had an army of incredible coaches and mentors around me since I started this journey. I have built and continue to work with a team of brilliant human beings. The clients I have had the privilege to work with are my inspiration. And yet, I'm honoured by the fact that whatever the results I have created and the contribution I have made thus far, while I certainly did not and could not have done it on my own, it all started with me. I am the source of my results, as you are the source of yours. I own that, and I want you to own that too. This will give you enormous power.

I realised early on in my journey that my focus was better placed not on changing the world but on changing myself. I wanted to learn how to own the power I felt deep inside and stay humble all at the same time. (This is a constant work in progress.)

From that realisation, I've faced down every single personal fear. A festering decades-long accumulation of lack of self-belief that paralysed me most mornings. The idea that I'm not good enough ran rampant through my brain until I strengthened my mental muscles enough to control and bring more understanding to those voices. This process cultivated a great sense of stillness inside, eventually opening me up to a deep 'knowingness' — that I can be, do, and have whatever my heart truly desires. I know this to be true about you too.

This didn't happen overnight. I have done the work. At the time of publishing, I have accumulated well over 20,000 hours of coaching, training, and development experience. Each and every single day, I spend on average two to four hours in my own personal processes and practices. I hired some of the best and most forward-thinking experts in the world to personally and professionally develop me, like Daniel

Priestley, co-author of *Key Person of Influence* (Rethink Press, 2015) who also wrote the foreword for this book and took my understanding of business to a whole other level; Gary John Bishop, author of *Unf*ck Yourself* (Yellow Kite, 2021), who stood for me no matter what over a four-year period in the early stages of my growth; Rich Litvin, co-author of *The Prosperous Coach* (Maurice Bassett, 2018), who transformed my independent coaching business in my first year back in 2017 and introduced me to the concept of high-fee; and many more incredible talents, some you will surely know of, others you never will, as they prefer to stay away from the spotlight. I've invested hundreds of thousands of dollars into my personal and professional development. The best money I've ever spent was investing in my personal growth — which is my number one value in life. I'm not a gambler, but I'll always bet on myself.

By cultivating what I'd later come to describe as an 'Unshakeable Belief' within myself, I have become unstoppable in pursuing my dreams, desires, and ambitions in building my business and creating my life, and I am completely unattached to any result. I'm committed, I trust, I am patient, and I am never attached. In the early days, this was frightening as I learned more and more how to confront my attachments, my shadows, and all that terrified me — it was anything but easy. My reward was liberation — a great sense of personal power, freedom, and peace within. And in more recent years, my reward was an increasingly profound realisation that life is best kept simple, relaxed, easy, and most of all, fun. Life, to me, is for enjoying while we have the chance.

I am a High-Performing Coach. In this book, I am going to show you how you can be one too.

I'd like to make a clear point: There's nothing particularly special about me in comparison to anyone else. I'm gifted in my own ways, as you are in yours. By Human Design, I am a Projector; by Astrology, I have five Leos in my chart (including the Sun). By the Gene Keys, my Siddhis include Humility, Stillness, and Universal Love. Studying these ancient wisdoms helped bring clarity to the darker, less conscious parts of me, like stress, bitterness, and arrogance, and validated what I had always felt deep inside, way beyond the shadows and struggles — that I was well and truly on my path doing what I was born to do. You have your own uniqueness just like me, and there's a perfect expression for the life you were born to live. Given that you are reading this, I trust you are on your path too. Today, perhaps one of the main differences between you and me is I've spent more 'time' — more time working on myself, more time coaching, and perhaps more time building out my business.

Of course, it's more than just 'time'; it's about the quality of the way we show up and engage in that time. If I could boil down the core qualities that have guided me and enhanced my time spent, they would be summarized as follows:

- The courage to always face myself and my fears
- The willingness to always believe in myself
- A relentless commitment to taking effective action
- Trust in the universe to always give me what I needed to grow
- The ability to look at myself and all my humanity, and to smile and laugh

This could all be summarized and boiled down into one single word: growth. Since 2009 I have valued my own personal growth as a human being above all else, and that will never stop — it simply takes different forms and shapes, the more growth that occurs. In the past, it was all about the 60-hour weeks of coaching and being coached. These days, it's more about free time, meditation, and solar gazing at sunset on the beach.

You'll see these values woven through the very fabric of this book, in every chapter, page, story, and word that is shared.

Through the experience, successes, failures (of which there have been many), and impacts I have had along the path, I discovered that there are Five Essential Elements to building a high-fee coaching business.

Unshakeable Belief

This Unshakeable Belief goes beyond just being confident, although that is also an outcome. It's about an enhanced level of awareness, presence, and the ability to think consciously from the heart and mind, with intention. The outcome is that you are left free, aligned, and unstoppable, no matter what stands in your way. This Unshakeable Belief also becomes yours to give away to your clients.

Business Foundations

To build something that will last, you must have the right foundations. Laying rock-solid Business Foundations in your coaching business will leave you feeling confident and at peace with what you have to offer, clear on how to express it, and so lit up about sharing it with the world that you simply can't shut up about it.

Breakthrough Process

We're not selling coaching, because coaching is not something that can be sold. The Breakthrough Process is a conversation that lets your potential clients experience the power of your coaching for themselves. They feel seen, gotten, and served, and free to choose to work with you or not.

Online Influence

You'll discover in this book that you really don't need a podcast, website, or a million followers on social media before you are able to create high-paying clients, and yet, in this day and age, building your Online Influence is absolutely essential to your long-term and sustainable success. Here, we get to break through even more of our own unconscious thinking, free ourselves up, and find effective and fun ways to express ourselves authentically, leaving people feeling that they know, like, and trust us.

Accountability & Coaching

Each of these elements are essential as described, but none more than Accountability & Coaching. In fact, being part of powerful, focused, and highly effective Accountability & Coaching accounts for 80 percent of your results. Without the right space in which to be held, supported, guided, trained, developed, and even pushed, in such a way that you have the experience that your feet are held to the fire, the past can often prevail, and you may easily slip back into your old ways of thinking and acting, which did not serve you. This is human nature.

The Five Essential Elements will take some effort to learn, develop, integrate, and master. They demand a great sense of tenacity, trust, and self-awareness if you choose to access them. And yet, with time, practice, and experience, before too long they begin to take shape and, just like riding a bike, one day you're doing it without even thinking.

The payoff? Nothing short of life-altering.

In this book we'll cover all this and more, including my highs, lows, struggles, and breakthroughs so that you, too, can discover how to do the same . . .

- Break through ...

- Build whatever you want to create in your life and your business, and ...

- Become a High-Performing Coach

It's actually very simple. Not easy, but simple.

1
Why I Became a Coach

To see truly and to be truly seen is a
most rare and precious gift.

It wasn't always this way.

My first thirty years on this planet were a combination of fun and adventure in my personal life and hopping from one career to the next in search of meaning. I had no clue what life was really about. Sure, I'd ticked the boxes of earning good money and some level of conventional 'white-collar' success, but nothing had made me feel deeply happy.

Was what I was getting out of bed for every morning truly worth it?

In the hunt for purpose and meaning, in my twenties I was stuck on a loop. I tried, failed, learned, tried again, and repeated this struggle countless times. I instinctively knew I had to keep going, but I won't lie: there were some really challenging times while I stumbled around in the dark, searching for the light — a light that finally shone in 2009 when I had a profound personal experience while walking through Bethnal

Green, East London, after a night out with my girlfriend at the time.

We were having 'one of those' arguments where I was (stupidly) convinced she was in the wrong and I was right and that's just how it was. I kept needling her and putting all my stuff on her, during which time she maintained: 'It's got nothing to do with me.'

She must have said this about twenty times over the course of this loop we were both stuck in, and she said it one final time ... 'It's got nothing to do with me.' I took a deep breath, dropped the idea that I was right, and allowed myself to wonder about a question that feels hilarious now, but it floored me back then and would change my life forever.

I said to myself, 'What if this has something to do with me?'

In a single moment, my whole life flashed in front of me.

Every argument I'd ever had.

Every failure, disappointment, relationship breakdown, and failed job or business venture.

Up until this moment, I'd always thought it was 'them' or 'that' — the world was at fault ... and yet, what I saw clearly was the single consistent factor. Me. It was all me.

I felt like I was going to pass out. I walked home. Alone. Entered my house, walked into my bedroom, and closed the door. In the minutes and hours that followed, I cried out the pain of thirty years of my BS.

The revelation was so painful that I sobbed for hours. And then after some time, the tears turned from devastation to what I'd later come to describe as transformation. My mind was blown, new space opened up, and I felt lighter, calmer, more peaceful. And the more space that opened up, the more I could see, feel, release, and let go of.

Insight after insight hit me like crashing waves — about my life, my family, my relationships, my mistakes, things I had done that I was not proud of, and how I'd been getting in my own way. Through all the tears, I felt awake for the first time in my life. Something powerful and very natural was building, and even though I had no idea what was happening to me exactly, I knew it was something beyond words ...

The next day, I had real conversations with my family for what felt like the first time in my life.

Through the tears, I said, 'I love you! So much! Why don't we ever tell each other we love each other? Why don't we talk about what happened back then?'

I connected to them on a level that was so deep and so nurturing to my soul. My honesty created a safe space for them to do the same. Admittedly, they were a bit freaked out by it all!

The very same day, I contacted all my ex-girlfriends and said I was sorry. Sorry for every fight, all the blame and delusion. Sorry for everything I did that did not work ...

I contacted other friends, colleagues, and relations from my past and started clearing up my part in situations that had been left incomplete.

I wrote a list and started cleaning up my entire life. Chasing money and status didn't fit any longer. I wanted my life to count for something. Whatever I was discovering was so important that I wanted to go deeper, discover more within myself, and share it with others.

All of this happened the next day.

I would wake up night after night, in cold sweats, crying from the dreams I'd just had, with another new insight about myself and my life that I would go on to handle and take care of as soon as I could.

I wanted to pay my dues. I wanted to make right every mistake I had made, intentionally or unintentionally. For example, one of first things I saw that I needed to do was to pay back the church. When I was a teenager, one of my first jobs was delivering a locally owned Catholic newspaper to people of that parish. Around the same time, an older boy I was running around with at the time disclosed how he used to 'skim' from his morning paper round.

'I take all the money every week and keep a few extra pounds for myself. No one ever notices, and you get some extra money.'

Sounded like a great idea to a young naïve kid who didn't have any money. So, I started skimming. One week a few quid, the next week a bit more, the next a bit more and more until it got to a point where I must have been pocketing half the money I was taking in. I was stupid to think that this would go unnoticed or was in any way justified. Men of faith can still do math. It didn't take long for the numbers to add up against me. After a few months of collecting the newspaper and my entitled tips, the Irish priest of the parish came up to me. It was an afternoon when I was to pick up the weekly papers. He handed me the newspapers and then pulled me aside.

He said, 'Ryan, we were doing the books and I noticed that there was quite a bit of money missing. Around £250, by our calculations.'

My heart leapt into my throat, but I tried to play it cool, as if I had no idea where it could be.

'Oh really? I'll go and check what I have at home', I said, knowing perfectly well where that missing money had gone: a box of change in my bedroom.

I was rattled; I had been caught. I couldn't let this weigh on me. The next day, I gathered all the coins that I hadn't spent, wrote a letter of resignation, and like a coward posted it through the letter box of the chapel house. As long as I lived there, I never returned. It has been a pockmark on my conscience ever since. It would play back in my memory over the years; however, I never did anything about it other than push it away.

Fast-forward some fourteen years, and here I was confronting all the demons, insecurities, and failures I had pushed down for so long. On the list of items I needed to resolve in order to settle my conscience, I booked a ticket home back to Scotland with a single intention of paying back the church. As soon as I got off the train, I went to the bank and collected £350 in cash. I figured the extra £100 was only fair, given interest and damage caused. I went to the chapel house where I used to go each week to collect the papers. I knocked on the door, nervous, and asked if the Irish priest was still here — I couldn't remember his name.

She directed me to him: 'Yes, Father Rihn is still here. He's in the confessional box.'

What a perfect place to say I'm sorry. I went into the confessional box, sat down on the little wooden stool, heavy with people's sins, and leaned into the little mesh window. I asked if I could come round the other side.

He said, 'Of course, my son.'

I rounded the confessional box and sat beside him. I looked him in the eyes for a moment. 'Father, can you remember many years ago there was a young boy with red hair who delivered the church paper, but he got into some trouble with the money he owed you and then he disappeared?'

He thought for a moment and said, 'Oh yes, I do remember that. Why do you ask?'

I said, with a choke in my throat, 'Father, that boy was me. I'm Ryan. And I wanted to tell you I'm so sorry for what I did and that I'm here to pay back what I owe the church.'

He took my hands, looked into my eyes, and said to me, 'Ryan, my son, we all make mistakes, and what counts is what we do about it. This is a very beautiful thing you have done today, and I want to thank you.' I cried.

I handed over the thick envelope of cash, and I felt lighter. In that moment, as in all the moments I put right, I got a little piece of my true self back. I'll never forget the grace and experience of forgiveness he gave me.

My new life was filled with moments like this — moments where I'd settle a piece of my past and reclaim my true and authentic self.

In the coming days, weeks, months, and years, I began to create my life versus merely reacting to whatever the world threw at me. I had never felt so powerful, purposeful, and free.

What happened that night in Bethnal Green?

What was the source of such a shift?

What inner process occurred that led to such radical new results?

I didn't have the words right away, and that was OK.

I later came to learn how to better articulate it.

There were four radical shifts that occurred in that instant that would change my life forever and that I have continued to cultivate and integrate from that day on. They are:

1. Authenticity — I was done pretending.

2. Responsibility — I was done being a victim.

3. Integrity — I was done dishonouring who I truly was.

4. Contribution — I wanted my life to be about something bigger than myself.

Two years on, my journey would eventually lead me to training and working with one of the world's leading organisations in personal development. **This is not just where I learned to be a great coach, it's also where I made sense of all that I had been going through on my own, and it's where I grew up.** For some five years, I dedicated 40–60+ hours a week towards my development. I was surrounded by world-class experts and remarkable human beings, guiding me and supporting me.

As my training developed, I began to coach doctors, therapists, psychologists, NLP Master Practitioners, and other coaches, Mums, Dads, brothers, sisters, successful high achievers, and those who wanted to be. I stood up on stages in front of hundreds of people and led hundreds of events. I moved to the States to take my training even further and was on a fast track like no other. It was equal parts terrifying and extraordinary.

Each and every day, I was held accountable for my own greatness. I spent a significant amount of my time absolutely humbled, on my knees emotionally, processing and confronting the darkest depths of my inner world, my stories, my fears, the remnants of my rigid mind, my need to be right … it was an exorcism of the highest order that I wanted more and more of. Fear, doubt, and illusion were wrung out of me. I was rebuilt. Starting anew.

In time, I began to push through and go way beyond my own limits. It was the biggest internal battle I'd ever faced. Until one day, I just couldn't see obstacles anymore. The phrases 'I can't' and 'It's not possible' were deleted from my personal lexicon. In their place were committed action and an internal belief structure that produced miracles for me.

Then the day came when I realised it was time to move on. I wanted more. More freedom, more impact, more financial freedom, and life on my terms. I wanted to build my own kingdom.

I returned to the UK with a vision that propelled me like the airplane to my future. It wasn't anything extravagant like working on a beach in Thailand at an expensive, luxurious hotel, which I obviously wouldn't mind. But the vision was simple.

Sitting in a coffee shop … Coaching my own clients … Life on my own terms is about having space, keeping things as simple as can be, being useful, and having fun. And giving away this Unshakeable Belief that I had developed inside.

Become a High-Performing Coach

In 2016, I found myself physically unfit. At this point I had dedicated a total of seven years to my mental, emotional, and spiritual strength and not my physical body's capabilities. I was called to move my ass! I found a passion for exercise and began dedicating most of my focus to my health — I became incredibly fit, doing burpees for fun. Before I knew it, I was working as an independent personal trainer in a gym and quickly built a successful business. Although it was satisfying to watch people transform their bodies — and their minds — through fitness, I missed coaching people through deeper work. I was a personal development junkie at heart. I began inviting my fitness clients to have a free personal development coaching session and created a few clients at £50/session.

After coaching for another organisation after so many years, I was finally coaching my own clients inside a coffee shop.

The dream had crystallised into reality in a very short time. Already, I wanted more.

I quickly realised that building a business, trading time for money was never going to satisfy the purpose, the mission, I felt growing inside me.

In 2017, my friend Natalia told me about a mutual acquaintance, Dan. She mentioned that Dan was doing insanely well. My ears perked up.

'How well?'

'Well, he's charging £2,500 for his coaching packages', she said.

'£2,500!!!???'

My brain exploded. Excitement, anger, and jealousy all emerged simultaneously. I didn't know whether to laugh or cry! And I thought to myself, *If he could charge that much, then so could I!*

What was Dan's secret? I got him on the phone the next day to find out.

'Dan, Natalia told me you're charging £2,500 for your coaching packages, and I'm charging £50! What am I missing!?'

He casually replied, 'Yes, that's right, I have a £2,500 coaching package and a £3,500 coaching package.'

'Dan, tell me, what do I have to do?'

'Ryan, read *The Prosperous Coach*.'

The moment I got off the phone, I got the book, read it cover to cover, and 48 hours later I'd booked a flight to LA to work with the author, Rich Litvin, and hire him as my coach.

In total, I needed around $20,000 to cover the training and trip to LA. This was money I did not have (I had just spent all my hard-earned cash on buying and renovating an apartment in London!). What I did have was an Unshakeable Belief that, with the right strategy, I could make that money back a thousand times over. With full conviction, I called my dad and the bank, and the money appeared in my account the very next day. The day after that, I invested it with Rich.

How did I feel?

Scared?

Nervous?

No.

I'm not going to lie to you — I was absolutely exhilarated!

A few weeks later, my first high-paying client signed up for a £1,600 coaching package. I had a feeling of shame in asking for such a high fee; my top lip trembled like a guilty man as I uttered those words for the first time: 'The investment to work with me is £1,600', but I pushed through it because, deep down, I knew this was right — for her and for me. To my surprise, she couldn't say yes fast enough and paid me right there and then. I hung up the call and thought to myself, "I could have charged more?!"

The next day I raised my fees to £2,500, then soon after to £3,500, then £4K. I had a wobble at £6K and went back down to £3,500K, then up to £10K. Soon enough I stopped working one-on-one and moved into high-fee group coaching. In the first four months alone of this experience, I would go on to create £60,000.

By 2019, I had a new inspiring vision: to help coaches build their business from the heart, as I had done. I quickly assembled a Co-Founding Team and High-Performing Coach was born. We would hit the seven-figure mark in less than two years.

What Excites Me About the Coaching Business

The estimated market size of the Coaching Industry for 2020 is $2.849 billion.[1]

According to PwC, the Coaching Industry is the second fastest growing sector in the world.

It is estimated that there were approximately 71,000 coaches worldwide in 2019, with about 92 percent of these active.

In 2019, the industry's trade group estimates that coaches have an average annual income ranging from $52,100 to $92,400.

Some specialty coaches can make much more, over $100,000.

This is very exciting for any coach committed to being an HPC!

However, what excites me most about building a coaching business is you've got to take yourself on. Becoming a coach is one of the most transformational personal development experiences you can embark on.

Building a coaching business is unlike any other.

- It's personal.

- It's intimate.

- It's vulnerable.

- It's real.

- It's fulfilling.

---

1 According to the 2020 ICF Global Coaching Study, the estimated global total coaching revenue in 2019 was $2.849 billion U.S., representing a 21% increase over the 2015 estimate.
(See book resources at www.ryanmathie.com/book for the ICF Study Executive Summary.)

The old sales strategies from the past won't work here. Authenticity is king. You get to show people how to be free — and for that to happen, you have to free yourself!

You've got to be the Real Deal. Take yourself on and deal with your fears, claim your power, express your gifts, and share it all with the world in a way that is aligned with the purity of your own heart. It's a process. It's a challenge. It needs an intelligent, tried and tested strategy. But what an opportunity. It's about your evolution!

I'm personally lit up that, by being a coach, you're not just building a business that can generate high revenue; you're making an impact through the difference you've made to yourself. It's self-sustaining and difference-making in every possible way. We talk a lot about changing the world — and I'll say it again ...

The most powerful way to change the world is to change yourself. It all starts with you ... and then you get to give it all away. What could be more magnificent?

I don't just invite my clients to step out and dream big; I've stepped out and dreamed big. I'm not just coaching our clients to take all those bold yet uncomfortable actions. I continue to take bold and uncomfortable actions, and I'll take them a million times over. I don't just ask my clients to take risks and spend money. I've taken the risks and spent the money.

And I don't do all these things once or twice, or last year or back then — I do it now, I'll do it all again tomorrow, and I'll do it over and over a million times as it's required of me, whatever it takes. This level of showing up is not a one-time gig. It's an ongoing phenomenon; it's a way of being and a way of life.

This is what being the Real Deal as a coach looks like.

I'm willing to do whatever is necessary to move beyond the limits of the mind and to think consciously from my heart and with intention. Sometimes this looks like having the courage to move mountains; other times it's about having the peace of mind to say and do nothing.

Have I arrived? No, I never will. Neither will you, because we are limitless, and there's always the next breakdown, the next breakthrough. It's an exhilarating ride, a mountain with no top, and we get to learn how to love the climb.

So yes, I'm excited about being a coach! But mostly I'm excited about the access it gives me to being alive.

The only limits are the ones we tell ourselves ...

For me, a coaching business is like no other.

It's about being fully alive, creating something on your terms, having a life of freedom as well as a life of impact. Deep down in our core, we all have a hunger to contribute and to help people, while also wanting to have a great life, all at the same time.

New coaches get stuck believing they have to choose between poverty and prosperity. Building your business in service to your clients is a powerful calling.

You want (and deserve) to create something incredible for yourself, your life, and your family too. Whether that's the freedom to travel, work remotely, or work 20 hours a week but still create a great income. Whatever it is that's important to you, a strong coaching business will deliver. Want to earn $10K/$20K+ a month and replace your old corporate income? That's very straightforward when you create high-paying clients.

Sometimes, depending on where we are on our journey, we still need to hear that permission from someone outside of ourselves to go forth and create what we desire. So, let's address this right now.

I am giving you permission *to give yourself permission* to ask for, go for, be, do, and have whatever your heart truly desires. Take a moment right now and give yourself permission to create the life that, right now, only exists in your wildest dreams. It may sound almost unbelievable, but believe it: life is good. It works in service of you, so believe it, be willing to believe it — heck, fake it if it gets you started — and in doing so you'll take a very powerful step towards making it a reality.

Any amount of money is possible in this business.

Our clients' fees range from $2.5K, $5K, $10K to $25K for a three- to six-month program. I have clients who charge $50K+ for a year's engagement. You can earn $5K per month, $10K, $20K, $30K — one of our clients recently had her first $50K month!

How did they do it?

By applying, learning, integrating, and allowing themselves to be used by the Five Essential Elements.

A Word on Money ...

When I talk about money, it's as a measure of two things: your impact as a coach and your personal growth. That's not the only way to measure these things, but your income is certainly one crucial and undeniable measure of them.

Some coaches have a hard time imagining high fees or making peace with the idea. They shy away from it or tell themselves it's not 'right' or that they don't deserve it.

Tell yourself you don't deserve it, and you'll create a matching reality. But what if it's not true ... What if you do deserve it? You can overcome this simply by allowing yourself to let in the idea you deserve every bit of joy, success, financial prosperity, and well-being that's available to you. In this universe, it is abundant, which means *you* are abundant, and your results can be limitless.

If you're not making much money as a coach, consider that there's something going on in the background that we need to distinguish. Usually, it's a set of misaligned thoughts and beliefs holding you back.

You won't be able to make the deep impact you crave if you aren't making enough to sustain yourself. There's a set of breakthroughs you need to have first. Your clients must pay you what you feel you're truly worth above and beyond your own limits, AND so they have skin in the game. The more they invest, the more they are invested, and the more they will show up and create great results because they're committed to their own dreams and desires too. And they want their money's worth!

All that we are discussing now points to the same thing: your breakthroughs. I/You/We get to break through whatever stands in our way and show our clients how to do the same. Be this kind of coach, and you can create ANY result in your business you want. Clients want to work with someone like that; wouldn't you?

What Drives Me

To set you up to start breaking through each and every barrier standing in your way, it will serve you to get connected to — and in touch with — what drives you, so I'll give you an example of what drives me.

For the first thirty years of my life, I was not doing work I loved. It was all about the money, and I let it take over. In my twenties I earned up to £100K some years in business-to-business roles and every day I was scheming how to get out. By the time I was thirty, I had probably tried and failed with 15, maybe 20, career or business ideas.

From being a DJ to being an actor to building my own juice company ... they all had various degrees of success, but none of them stuck.

Why?

Because at some point I would always start telling myself I wasn't good enough. As soon as it started to get hard, I'd always end up in the same place: in my head — where doubt would take over. Then I'd quit and move on to the next idea. I was constantly searching for something I was good enough at. Of course, the truth was I was good at all of it; I just didn't believe that. My belief in myself was the polar opposite of unshakeable.

Yet in spite of this, I was frustrated because I knew I wasn't fulfilling my potential. It broke my heart because deep down, beyond the doubt and fear, I knew I had so much inside of me to give. It was all a beautiful, messy process to guide me to where I belonged: right here.

Today, I deliver breakthroughs to the world in a way that has been described as powerful, gentle, direct, playful, remarkably simple, profound, and from the heart. It juices me up so much that I bounce out of bed in the morning. OK, to be totally honest, that's not exactly accurate — my mind and heart bounce out of bed, and my body catches up eventually!

Today, what drives me is the commitment to being my true, authentic, aligned, and brilliant self, living out a life that I can be proud of and grateful for SO THAT I can share anything of value to any and all who want to hear it. To summarise, what drives me is the opportunity to contribute to you. You are my muse.

What Drives You?

Knowing there was more inside of me I wanted to access — and that there's more to come — is also what drives me. That doesn't necessarily mean Batman-style heroics, Ferraris, and dollar signs. It's much deeper than that. It's about an ever-greater sense of peace inside my mind and joy in my heart. Serenity, calm, and simplicity in life ...

Take a moment now and see if my story relates to you, or if yours looks a bit different. Get in touch with what's driving you.

Why are you here?

Maybe on one level, it's about making a difference, but why do you want to make a difference?

Or maybe you want to build a $250,000-a-year coaching business, but why do you want to do that?

Exercise:
Seven Layers Deep

I invite you at this point to go seven layers deep. This is an exercise to connect to your why, to get you connected to what's driving you.

I want you to ask yourself, 'Why am I here reading this book?' Then I want you to answer, and then ask the same question, 'Why?', seven times.

For example:

I am reading this book because I want to learn about how to build a coaching business.

Why?

Because I want to learn how to create an impact and make a great living too.

Why?

I want to create an impact and make a great living too because I want to live fulfilled.

Why?

I want to live fulfilled so that I can feel proud of myself.

Why?

Because I spent the majority of my life hiding and not going for what I truly wanted and being ashamed, and I've gotten to a stage in my life now where I am no longer willing to do that.

Why?

I am no longer willing to do that because I get that I have nothing to be ashamed of.

Why?

Because I am perfect, wonderful, infinitely powerful, and I can have the life I want, and I'm going to have it, that's why!

If you ask yourself those questions in that way, seven times, you'll get a greater sense of what's driving you and why you're here. Take a few moments now and see where you go.

Tip: Don't get hung up on trying to get this right. Just let the questions and answers flow and allow your heart to speak. If possible, it can be more helpful to have someone else ask you the question seven times.

2
Where Are You Now?

The quality of your thinking and acting
creates the quality of your results.

When we start working with new coaches, the first step is to establish where they are now, what their motivation is, what they're committed to, and what their current strategy is.

That conversation is always revealing. It shows how far they have come — their strengths, weaknesses, and limitations — and starts to uncover everything under the surface. Then we dive deep into what's getting in the way of them creating the results they really want.

We, as humans, have a fantastic talent in talking to ourselves in such a way that makes simple problems seem complex.

Trying to Reinvent the Wheel
(And doing things that don't really
work for longer than is necessary)

There are two pillars to creating extraordinary results ...

Your beliefs (how you talk to yourself) and your strategy (what you do or don't do).

Beliefs are what we create through our thinking, internally. The strategy is what we implement through action, externally.

As a new coach looking to learn how to create high-paying clients, it goes without saying that you haven't built a successful coaching business before, which means you don't know the strategy. You might engage in a trial-by-error approach, which is certainly one way of doing things, but this approach is inconsistent with what coaching is really all about. You might copy people online, assuming that what you are mimicking is effective, or you might be doing dead-end tasks you think will work, like inviting people to like your Facebook page, posting fancy quotes, or working tirelessly on your branding even though you are not engaged in any client-creating strategies. One of my newer clients explained to me how she was struggling for time, and I asked her to share with me what was in her schedule. She had three hours a week dedicated to admin and finance-related tasks to which I reminded her, 'You're not making any money yet. Delete this from your schedule and apply the Breakthrough Process instead!' She created her first high-fee client at £3,000 a few days later.

Spinning. Ineffective strategies. Busywork. I know it all too well, having been through it myself.

When I started out, I shared on Facebook that I was now building my coaching business. Do you know what happened? Nothing.

I shared my 'why'.

Crickets ...

I posted a blog. Nada.

I updated my profile information. Zip.

I frequently checked the number of likes and refreshed my inbox and yes, you guessed it ...

I ticked all those boxes for two whole weeks, and then on Sunday morning as I brushed my teeth, I looked at myself in the mirror and said out loud, *Ryan, you have no idea what the heck you're doing.*

This realisation was so powerful because the next thought was a game-changer: *I need to hire a coach!* Two weeks later, I heard about Dan, an acquaintance I had coached years before, then Rich, and the high fees they were earning, and shortly after that, I hired my coach. Coincidence? No. I got powerfully straight with myself and generated a greater quality of thinking, which opened me and the world up in a multitude of ways. All I had to do was walk through the doors I was asking to be opened.

Because I've struggled with, and broken through, the same challenges most new coaches face, I can help them get real with the fact that they — like me, at that point — don't know how to build a coaching business and guide them towards what makes the biggest difference.

Depending on an individual's level of awareness, admitting you don't know everything or that you need help can be quite the task, and it's essential if you want to become a High-Performing Coach. A coach who chooses to struggle with the same problem for long is not an example to themself or to their clients. A coach, on the other hand, who understands and believes in the power of coaching knows that the most effective way to solve a problem is to hire an expert to show you how. And further still, a coach who goes beyond knowing, into aligned action, will seek out the best help they can find and cause a breakthrough for themself in whatever area they are stuck in.

It's OK to not know.

It's OK to not have it all figured out.

It's OK to be exactly where you are, and to consider that where you are at right now is absolutely perfect.

It's OK to feel unsure or scared.

This level of acceptance can help you stop living in denial, wasting precious time, or thinking it's going to work out because you put up a website. It's more than that.

Your challenges can be effectively solved with the right training and support. On the other side of your breakdown is the next breakthrough, if you so choose it to be.

Make it your job to be an example to your clients and do exactly what you would recommend they do. Over and over.

You have a challenge? *Break through it.*

Recognise the need for help? *Find the best help you can.*

Tempted to use 'money' as an excuse? *Get that you are worth the best, and that with the best help and application of the training, you'll create results, breakthroughs, and enormous wealth worth way more than your original investment.*

Invested before and it didn't work out? *Don't let that be a great excuse to stop now. Learn from the experience and try again.*

Five Core Barriers All Coaches Face

Although there is a multitude of different challenges, I usually see them boil down into five core barriers. You may be dealing with one, two, three, four, or all five.

Core barrier #1: False/limiting/unconscious beliefs

Some specific beliefs hold coaches back the most. These beliefs are usually split into three categories: beliefs about themselves, their clients, and their business.

A. Your beliefs about yourself:
    'I'm not a good enough coach. I need more training. I'm not worth a high fee. My coaching won't be effective. What if I fail?'
B. Your beliefs about your clients:
    'My potential clients will think I'm being salesy. Clients don't want to hear from me. Clients won't pay for coaching, and they certainly won't pay a high fee!'
C. Your beliefs about your own business:
    'My business won't succeed. My business can't generate sustainable amounts of revenue. It's just not going to work out!'

These beliefs become your world — a 'reality' you can't escape. It limits the actions you can take. When feeling anxious and frustrated, it will look like everything outside yourself is in your way, but it's actually the internal walls you've unconsciously put up and created in your own mind.

Coaches with limiting beliefs and thought processes such as these will never reach the point where they can effectively use tools, strategies, or programs because they'll stop themselves before they get close enough.

They'll use money as an excuse. If they believe they're going to fail, they won't allow themselves to spend money on something that won't succeed. They might often fall into the trap of the blame game, finding fault with their circumstances, training, coach, the program they're in ... clutching at the external — anything on the surface level — but what's underneath all the stories is their own fear of failure, fuelled by a set of limiting beliefs that they perpetuate.

It's paralysing.

With Unshakeable Belief, your views, opinions, and beliefs are consciously and deliberately guided towards those thoughts that are a match for the results you want — creating your own reality and allowing yourself to thrive.

Core barrier #2: I don't know the business of coaching

I haven't found my niche.

I can't seem to get my messaging right.

I charge per hour because that's what I was told to do in my training.

My fees are low because that's the going rate.

I don't really have my own unique process or signature program.

When you have never built a successful coaching business before and no one has effectively shown you how, if you're not careful, you can easily enter the lost world of trying to reinvent the wheel.

Understanding and setting solid Business Foundations can be one of the most challenging barriers for new coaches if these steps are not approached in a strategic way.

When the Business Foundations are not laid intelligently, the impact can often feed a lack of confidence that becomes like a vicious cycle, feeding more and more into those limiting beliefs ...

I started off charging a low fee. I didn't even understand the word 'niche'. We all have to start somewhere, but if we want to build something truly great, we need rock-solid Business Foundations (or rock-solid enough!) to get out there and do the real work of coaching people and building the business at a much higher level.

Core barrier #3: I don't know how to create high-paying clients

> Where are all the clients? How do I find them?
>
> Where are the high-paying ones? I just keep finding the low-paying ones.
>
> What should I say? What should I do? What process should I follow?
>
> How do I leave clients wanting to work with me?
>
> How do I make my offer?
>
> How do I respond to 'No, it's too expensive', 'I can't afford it', or 'I need to talk to my partner?'

As soon as I realised I needed to learn the strategy to build the business, initially I felt deflated … It hit me that I had to learn something new all over again. I'd spent years mastering the art and craft of coaching and thought I was good to go, but I wasn't. In truth, I was only halfway there. Then I had a more useful and exciting thought: "What if I got as good at the business of coaching as I am at the coaching itself?"

Where clients are, how to find them, how to speak to them, how to actually have someone say yes — this is a real challenge, and without having a deeper understanding of what it really takes, it can leave most coaches completely defeated, scratching their heads and wondering what they're missing.

What they're missing is a process that turns every person into a potential client, every conversation into the opportunity to make a difference, and every 'No way, I simply don't have that kind of money' into the perfect environment for the breakthrough of your client's life.

Not knowing how to handle what I refer to as 'the money conversation' was, for me, the single most frustrating experience. After all that effort and all that work, only to experience this time and time again … Yet, in the end, I turned this into my greatest opportunity. I began using the experience to figure something out — how to help my clients have a breakthrough instead — and say YES to working with me, say yes to their life! You'll be learning how in this book.

Core barrier #4: Lack of visibility online

> I haven't announced I'm a coach yet to my network.
>
> I haven't told my current employer, so I'm staying offline for now.
>
> I'm frightened I'll get judged.
>
> I don't know how or where to post content.
>
> I don't want to jump on the bandwagon and use social media.

I don't do social media.

I'm doing it, but it's not really my thing.

I'm doing it, but it's not really working.

I don't want to be out there chasing people and looking like one of those desperate coaches I see posting videos all the time!

This type of thinking feeds the low-vibrational, shakeable belief system, not to mention keeps you far, far away from your clients and getting you, your message, and your gifts out there in the world.

The truth is that behind and underneath all of these concerns is fear. Fear of failure, fear of getting it wrong, fear of being judged, fear of being laughed at, and so on.

In the early days, I scheduled three Facebook Lives over a three-day period. I was taking coaches through the Unshakeable Belief training; this was before the days of HPC.

I remember on day 1, I was so nervous I couldn't eat or drink, and that was hard because the Facebook Lives were scheduled for 2 pm!

In spite of all my training and readiness, I still had all those familiar bodily sensations and thoughts, which I observed and let do what they had to do, without letting it stop me. I did enough to push through, and 10 minutes into my Live, I was flowing.

On day 2, it was similar, but I could drink. Five minutes into the Live and I was flowing.

On day 3, I had breakfast and enjoyed a coffee, and I experienced no nerves on the build-up to the training.

Once you clear away all the limiting thoughts around how to show up, and you attain a deeper understanding of how to create content that actually connects on social media, you will begin to create online influence, grow your network, and magnetically attract more people towards you.

Core barrier #5: Working in isolation

> I'm not sure if what I'm doing is working.
>
> I'm getting distracted by other things.
>
> I seem to be less productive on my own.
>
> I miss working in a team. It's a little lonely out here!
>
> I do meet regularly as part of a mastermind group. It's nice to connect, but the trouble is that they're not doing so well either!
>
> I wish I had someone to assure me I'm on the right track. I don't know what I'm getting wrong.
>
> Today I'm working on my logos, and tomorrow I think I'll go meet a friend for a coffee ... I need a break! But I'm feeling guilty about that too.

Without working in the right environment, low or no performance can quickly become the new norm and, in some cases, become like the blind leading the blind. It's great to stay connected to your peers but, in most cases, that by itself is not a space that will bring about radical shifts in your performance.

Most of us are used to working in teams. Then all of a sudden to be 'alone', trying to work it all out as a solo-preneur brings about even more challenges.

We, humans and coaches alike, thrive in powerful Accountability & Coaching. Accountability & Coaching hold us to our word, support us through our blocks, and empower breakthrough results. Each and every one of our most successful clients was someone who understood the power of this and was quite willing to admit they wanted and needed a kick up the you-know-what!

The Ultimate Breakdown

Some coaches manage to do OK but fall quite short of the mark they had imagined for themselves. Many coaches get stuck, lean on their partner for financial support, run low on savings, take part-time work, and consider going back to their old career.

Any negative belief that you held about not being good enough will get reinforced more and more thanks to a lack of results. You feel like you have no control ... don't know what to do ... and you're in your head.

It's ineffective. It's frustrating. It's scary.

You're in total breakdown. This is the bad news, but there is light inside the darkness. While all of this is certainly a struggle, your breakdown is also a perfect storm for breakthroughs so long as you stick it out and push through to the other side. At this critical crossroads you have two choices ...

Give up. Let go of the dream of building your own business. Maybe work as a coach inside someone else's business or go back to the old career you swore you'd never return to.

Or ...

Break through.

Wherever you're at, I know you want to break through something, so let's continue …

RED-AMBER-GREEN

Let's take a quick test and see where you are right now against the Five Essential Elements of building your business to profitability:

- Unshakeable Belief

- Business Foundations

- Breakthrough Process

- Online Influence

- Accountability & Coaching

Read the following statements and give yourself a Red, Amber, or Green for each — Red being nonexistent, Amber being somewhat existent, and Green being fully existent.

Your responses will indicate and begin to shine a light on where you are, your strengths, and your areas for development.

> **Unshakeable Belief:** I have Unshakeable Belief in myself and my ability to build the coaching business I have been dreaming about.
>
> Is this nonexistent, somewhat existent, or fully existent?
>
> Red, Amber, or Green?
>
> **Business Foundations:** My Business Foundations (Niche, Messaging, Method, Program, Fees) are clear, solid, developed, and fully optimised to build a high-fee online coaching business.

Is this nonexistent, somewhat existent, or fully existent?

Red, Amber, or Green?

Breakthrough Process: I follow a clearly defined process for creating clients, have a consistent flow of enrolment calls, and 25–50 percent or more of my calls result in a high-fee client.

Is this nonexistent, somewhat existent, or fully existent?

Red, Amber, or Green?

Online Influence: I show up freely and consistently online. My audience is growing, and being online is an effective source of call bookings for my coaching business.

Is this nonexistent, somewhat existent, or fully existent?

Red, Amber, or Green?

Accountability & Coaching : I am invested in and part of a powerful accountability, training, and development structure led by experts in building a profitable coaching business.

Is this nonexistent, somewhat existent, fully existent?

Red, Amber, or Green?

Your colours will be revealing.

The answer to where many of your gaps lie is in front of you.

We are beginning to demystify the source of your results (or lack of).

No matter how you fared for each element, this is only a measure of where you are now, not where you are headed if you follow and apply the ideas laid out in this book.

Circle back at the end of the book and take the test again. You'll be amazed to see how far you've come through this process alone.

Vision, Mission, and Values

Vision

Here's a question for you ...

What is the change you want to see in the world?

This vision of a new world is not something you have to realise all alone (we'll come to your part next). For now, simply get in touch with the change you want to see and write it down.

Our vision at HPC is that coaching, therapy, and personal development in all of its forms become as indispensable as running water, electricity, and Wi-Fi in every home, workplace, school, and hospital.

Mission

Next, what's your mission? What part will you play directly in bringing this vision for a better world to life?

Take a moment now, get in touch with it, and write it down.

Our mission at HPC is to develop coaches to become personally successful, excellent examples of human potential, confident in their ability to make a difference in a positive way and go and make that difference.

Values

Now let's get clear about your three core values.

You might want to write down a few and circle your top three.

Don't go to lists for this. I invite you simply to get in touch with the three that are most important to you right now — this is very personal. What's most important to you? Get connected to your top three.

Our core values at HPC are as follows: be courageous, be yourself, and lead from the heart.

Results

Now, inspired by your own vision for the change in the world you want to see, motivated by your mission in making that change, and influenced by your core values, let's get in touch with the results you want to create from all that!

Let's look three years into the future — feel free to look twelve months ahead, five years ahead, ten years ahead, whatever you prefer — and consider this ...

What would be possible for you if you showed up completely aligned with your vision, mission, and values; had Unshakeable Belief, rock-solid Business Foundations, and the right strategy; knew how to create high-paying clients; were creating influence online; and had Accountability & Coaching to support you that is a match for what you set out to accomplish?

If you had ALL this in place, where would you be in the next twelve months? Three years? Five years? That's what we want to do now. Take a moment and allow yourself to get present to the results you want to create, because that's the single and sole purpose of this book — you creating the results you really want and are capable of. I promise if you allow yourself to step into this exercise and follow this book's coaching, you will have those results and more.

In 2017, I created a vision for a coaching business generating £350K per year that helped people become unstoppable. That seemed almost hard to believe, but I chose to believe it anyway!

Fast-forward, and HPC is now a fast-growing, seven-figure global online business. I made this happen by rigorously applying every single idea laid out in this book. In this time, I've also mentored thousands of coaches of all backgrounds and all ethnicities, with a wide range of experiences, to go from low/no fee to $5K, $10K, $20K, or $50K per month.

What's your vision for the world, personal mission, and core values?

What's your vision for yourself, your life, AND your coaching business ... ?

What income would you love to earn?

3
The Five Distinctions of a High-Performing Coach

Seeing is not fixed; seeing is a conscious creation.

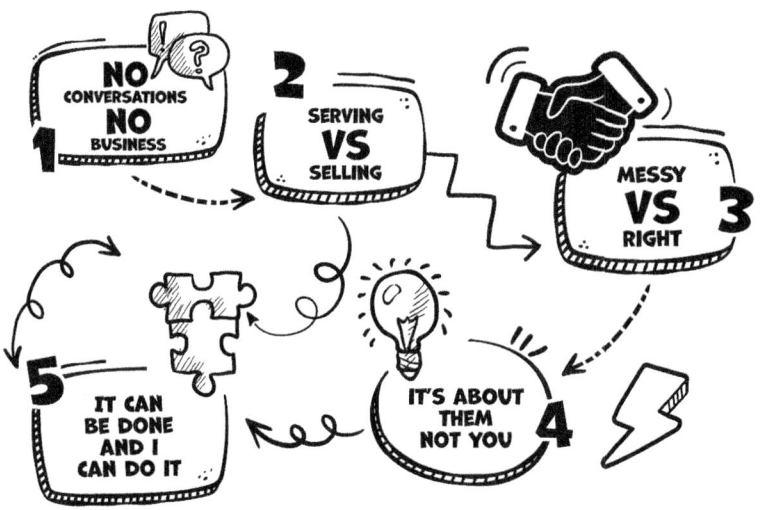

Sobiya had a big vision, but an equally strong limiting belief was holding her back.

'I had an intense desire to create a successful coaching business, work with high-performing individuals, and create impact in the world. I felt frustrated because I didn't know how to take action and make this a reality.

'I was working with one client in person, at a rate of £45 an hour. If I had continued in that direction, I would still be working as a teacher, and I wouldn't have a successful coaching business.'

She struggled with selling vs. serving and feared being viewed as a sleazy saleswoman. Before she could move forward, she needed to make a key distinction between the idea of selling vs. the power of serving.

'Being a high achiever, I always wanted things to be "perfect" and "right," but that was impossible, and it would leave me feeling stuck and frustrated.'

Personally, I'd learned to sidestep the 'perfect' trap (which I'll share more about in the next section), so it was easy for me to see clearly why she was getting stuck and exactly how to get her unstuck through the power of Unshakeable Belief and the Five Distinctions of an HPC.

What Is a Distinction?

A distinction is, to a coach, what a hammer is to a carpenter.

A distinction is a lens, and it changes the way we look at something. It's a distinct way of looking at a problem or situation. It's an idea — a tool — that coaches apply to themselves and their clients.

What Are We Applying, and Why Are We Applying It?

Adjusting your perception will alter how you think and feel about situations and the actions you then take, influencing the outcome. That's what we want. We want to create outcomes, but not any old outcomes. We must focus on the outcomes we want for ourselves, our business, and our clients, and doing it in a way that creates breakthroughs. This is when you step into being the creator of your own reality.

Your actions and your entire way of showing up all come from your thinking. The way you see the world alters your thinking. Whether you call this interpretation, decisions, opinions, fixed ideas, views, or beliefs, once it goes through the factory in your brain, it all comes out to the same point: thoughts.

To influence the quality of our thinking, we must learn to influence the quality of our seeing.

To demonstrate how this works, you had a thought about this book, which made you buy it and begin reading. Perhaps you thought it would make a difference in your coaching business. In your perception, the book looked like it could help you, and now here we are, over a quarter of the way through, with lots of new openings and insights, I am sure.

This kind of thinking came from an open mind and open heart. It is the kind of thinking that I describe as quality, high-vibrational thinking that allows for something new to enter and impact you in a positive way.

What do I mean by high-vibrational? *Ask and It Is Given* by Esther and Jerry Hicks (Hay House, 2004) is the best work I have ever encountered on the concept of energy: high-vibration, low-vibration, and the law of attraction.

In summary, everything is energy. The energy either feels good or it doesn't. Try telling yourself how awful you are and how nothing you are going to take on is going to turn out. It won't feel good — this is low-vibrational thinking and speaking. With a deeper understanding that you will gain from this book, you can learn to feel into high-vibrational thinking, as a kind of wake-up call to your unconscious patterns.

Try telling yourself how everything is going to turn out: you're exactly where you need to be, you are capable, deserving, worthy ... That messaging feels beyond good. This is high-vibrational thinking and speaking.

Conversely, had you first looked at this book and engaged in a negative thought process about it, which by nature is of a lower vibrational energy — perhaps you decided it wasn't going to be helpful, perhaps judging the book itself by the cover — well, we wouldn't be here together right now. Everything would have changed ...

High-vibrational, high-quality thinking attracts high-vibrational and quality things, people, and experiences. Low-vibrational, low-quality thinking attracts low-vibrational and low-quality things, people, and experiences.

This is the power of thought, and this is the universal law of attraction explained in a nutshell. I say universal because it's not an idea; it's science. The quality of your thinking mind alters EVERYTHING.

When we consciously apply a distinction in our lives, businesses, or coaching conversations with our clients, we get to influence those thoughts. It's like our hands are put firmly on the driving wheel. We're no longer subjected to unconscious thinking, spiralling downwards, leaving us feeling scared, sad, or defeated, wondering why we're not creating results. We now know how to influence our response — our thoughts, feelings, and actions. We know how to affect results by applying a powerful distinction. We know how to deliberately and quite effortlessly think better quality and more intentional thoughts.

Now, let's jump into the Five Distinctions of a High-Performing Coach.

The Five Distinctions of a High-Performing Coach

Distinction 1: No Conversations, No Business

This week, with how many people did you share what you're up to in your life, and your vision and mission?

This week, how many conversations did you have about your coaching business?

This week, how many conversations did you intentionally lead that gave someone a sense of what it's like to work with you?

This week, how many conversations did you lead that were meaningful to someone, leaving that person open and wanting more?

This week, how many conversations did you have that created a clear pathway for someone to be able to continue that conversation with you, excited to go even deeper?

If your answer is many, few, or none, notice how that's been affecting your results.

Consider this idea: no conversations, no business.

Your business is built upon conversations. It's simply a function of talking to people. No conversations, no business.

If you have a referral-based business only, you might see results; however, you have no control. We want to be in control of our business. If you are generating referrals, that certainly points to the quality of your work, but it also shows that your business is in the control of others, and that's not a business that you can rely on. I invite you to see referrals as the icing on the cake, rather than the whole cake itself, and to get in control of your business by generating intentional, meaningful, and powerful conversations every week.

I created this distinction after an insight one day as I was tracking my own data. The weeks in which I had generated lots of conversations with potential clients were followed by weeks that flowed with new clients. Weeks when I didn't have conversations with potential clients resulted in no clients, or a very low number, in comparison.

Without the distinction of 'No conversations, no business', you'll possibly fall into the trap of sitting there waiting and hoping for clients to come. Social media content can be a huge source of creating connections and new clients, and for some, this might be enough based on your goals and your results. However, this approach can often take some time before you start seeing any results at all — if ever! If you want results fast and you want to maximise the opportunity of your coaching business, you'll want to generate conversations directly in parallel to other strategies. This is particularly important during the launch phase of your coaching business as it will really get things moving.

'No conversations, no business' is intended to give you the understanding that you're the source of your business. Once you get this, you can go and start creating results with velocity. The most important thing to understand is that business is done through the power of conversations. If you are not having conversations, there won't be a coaching business.

We might be distracted by all the complicated methods of digital marketing, funnels, and podcasts. When you're new to the industry, these 'shiny new objects' feel like the golden ticket. The truth is, I've not met many new coaches who are in the launch phase of their business — anywhere from the first six months to three years (everyone moves at different pace) — who created results by working with expensive systems and marketers too early on in their process. These scaling tactics are best implemented when we've laid the groundwork; have tried, tested, and validated our business; and have something to scale.

A brand-new coach or underperforming coach doesn't necessarily need any of these complicated methods at this stage, if ever! Being armed with the understanding that you need to have conversations, and having enough skill in how to lead those conversations and clarity on where you can have them, will open up the opportunities right in front of you and leave you free to generate coaching opportunities almost at will.

No conversations, no business. Allow this distinction to give you power. If it makes you feel in any way uncomfortable, recognise it's because the reality is kicking in that you have to do something new that's bumping up against a limiting belief about you, your clients, or your business.

No conversations, no business. One person to another, one at a time. Sounds so simple — and it is! Conversations are also far more powerful and effective for a new coach than any online funnel, which will take a lot of time, energy, money, and skill, because having a conversation is something you can do today, right now, for free.

In the upcoming chapters, we'll dive deep into what to say and how the conversation can go. For now, just let in this idea: it's all in your control, through your speaking, and if you're not speaking about your coaching in an effective way — yep, you guessed it — no business.

Looking at your business through the distinction of No conversations, no business, what starts to open up for you? What new actions do you see to take? How do you feel? What thoughts appear? Are they low- or high-vibrational? Unshakeable or shakeable? True or false? Useful or not?

Distinction 2: Serving vs. Selling

This one is straight out of Rich Litvin's playbook, and I just absolutely loved it.

Serving vs. Selling breaks through the concern that if you start talking to people, they're going to think you're being salesy. This is a concern shared by the vast majority of coaches new to the industry. I felt the same at the start. 'Salesy' is the last thing you want associated with your good name.

Truth is, you don't want to sell anything anyway; you want clients who want what you have to offer, so it feels like a collaboration rather than a transaction. What you want is to make a difference ... to serve ... and this is why this distinction is so powerful. It's grounded in truth.

You can't sell high-fee coaching. Just try, and you'll see potential clients run for the hills. Coaching is too personal, too intimate; it requires human-to-human, heart-to-heart connection. The second you try to sell it, you'll be met with resistance.

The better path to take is to give people a powerful experience: a life-changing conversation that makes a difference in your clients' lives. In other words, be a coach in each and every conversation you have with your potential clients and, with permission if needed, serve them. Therefore, you fulfil the whole reason you wanted to become a coach in the first place, which is to make a difference. To coach.

Serving vs. Selling is a breath of fresh air. This is the truth. What is not the truth is that you're trying to sell anybody anything. Getting caught up in the idea that others may think you are selling something is simply not useful and will only get in your way of serving!

Looking at your potential clients through the distinction of Serving vs. Selling, what starts to open up for you? What new actions do you see to take? How do you feel? What thoughts appear? Are they low- or high-vibrational? Unshakeable or shakeable? True or false? Useful or not?

Distinction 3: Messy vs. Right

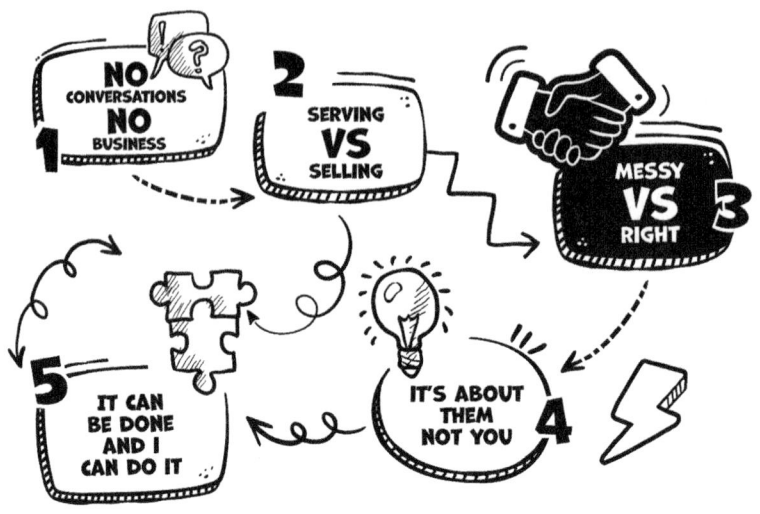

This is a distinction that I practised unconsciously for years after I was tired of trying to get things perfect. I noticed that whenever I had an event or presentation I was leading, through all my different careers, I would spend a lot of time trying to get it perfect. I would write scripts. I would put so much pressure on myself to perform in a certain way. But I would be filled with anxiety in the days leading up to the event.

It was horrible. I felt overwhelmed and under a lot of pressure. I didn't enjoy the process. In the end, I found that once I let all of that go, I'd get into a flow, and everything I wanted to say came naturally.

I realised what was going to be better for me was to permit myself to be a little bit messy, to give myself a bit of grace, especially at the start of a new journey.

Messy vs. Right is about permitting yourself to play. If you imagine when you were a kid and you had your brand-new white shirt on, or new pink dress, for many of us, your mum really cared that you didn't get it dirty. But all you cared about was playing. Your mum might have even gotten a little stressed, but you were having loads of fun. Or maybe you were the kid trying to keep yourself clean and it got in your way of having fun? That's what it's about. We miss that opportunity to enjoy the process when we try to stay perfect.

Of course, all that pressure of trying to get it right affects our performance and the experience others have of us, too. Allowing yourself to get a bit messy changes the experience and gives you more freedom. You can just show up and be free. People love to be around someone who can show up like this: present.

When you do this, you get to express a part of yourself that is highly attractive — presence is high-vibrational, and freedom is hot! People want that. It's not just a great experience for you to show up and allow yourself the freedom to not get it right or perfect, but it's a great experience for the people engaging with you, because they get to experience it for themselves too. This attractive quality invites in so much fun and magic. And you'll be utterly amazed how well you do and what you create from this kind of space. Ruminate on Messy vs. Right. What new actions do you see to take? How do you feel? What thoughts appear? Are they low- or high-vibrational? Unshakeable or shakeable? True or false? Useful or not?

Distinction 4: It's About Them, Not You

For many of the coaches I have worked with, this distinction has been a game-changer. It's about them, not you.

At the start of my coaching business journey, I was so committed to the difference I wanted to make that my 'stuff' simply wasn't there. I didn't make it about me, my fears, the money, what they would think, and so on. I was so in it for them, and it gave me an enormous amount of power. The coaches who end up most stuck are working through their fears, their concerns about their reputation, what people will say, what if it doesn't work, what if they fail, what if they get judged ... They're making it all about them. Carrying very heavy energy like this won't lend itself to being what is required to shine that light you want to shine!

And when it's about you in this way, you often don't even get out of the gate because you're so concerned about your-self. You're so concerned about how you feel, what they're going to think, or what others will say. You're so concerned that you make your own world so small and limiting that you miss the big picture. The big picture is all of that contribution that you are here to make. Allow yourself to embrace this idea, to let go of your concerns and your fears and all of the things that you're struggling with. Instead, get your focus on the contribution and the difference that you want to make. Has it been about them, not you? Shift it around. It's about them, not you! That distinction is going to give you all the space in the world to show up and serve your clients.

There's a lot of mastery in this simple idea because it's easy to get caught up thinking about our problems. But those thoughts just take us out of the game. They take you away from what you want to do, which is to coach and make a difference in people's lives. These concerning thoughts can happen so quickly that you don't even know you've spent the last day, week, month, or year caught up in them. You're living in this negative world that is all made up in your mind and disconnects you from what you're committed to as a coach, as an entrepreneur, as a human being.

It's about them, not you! This distinction is about the ability to observe yourself and start catching yourself when you're making it about you. Procrastinating is a sign of that. Negative feelings are another. When you get caught up in that space, then you're making it about you. You need to be vigilant about these thoughts and then bring yourself right back to the idea that it's not about you; it's about your clients.

If you put your focus on your clients, versus on you, you and your concerns are going to disappear, and you'll be left feeling free and motivated to act in service of them. You are whatever you say you are. You really do get to say who you are, what you'll think, and who you'll be. This is just another skill that, in time and with practice, you can master. And as you practise this distinction, you're going to be left more and more inspired to take all the necessary actions required to show up for your clients and do your thing. It's liberating when it's not all about you.

As you allow yourself to get present to the difference you are here to make — and apply the idea that it's about them, not you, what new actions do you see to take? How do you feel? What thoughts appear? Are they low- or high-vibrational? Unshakeable or shakeable? True or false? Useful or not?

Distinction 5: It Can Be Done, and I Can Do It

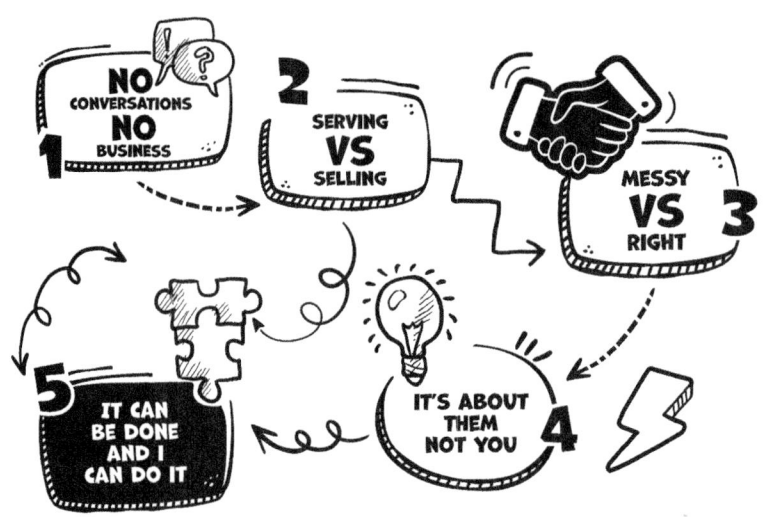

This distinction is about taking on any false idea that something is not possible for you. However, if you believe it's possible for you, you'll be able to think, feel, and act in alignment with that. Then you'll create results that are also in alignment with your thinking. If you believe you can't do it, then you won't get out of the gate. If you believe you can't do it, then you'll just find excuse after excuse. If you believe you can't do it, then you'll find evidence all over the place to back up your belief that you can't do it.

The truth is that it can be done. And you can do it. If you allow yourself to take that on, then nothing will get in your way. You will be unstoppable. You will be free to just keep taking as much action as necessary. You'll believe in yourself as a coach. You'll believe in yourself and the business that you're building, and you'll believe in yourself as a human being out there who is contributing to the world. *It can be done, and I can do it.* Write it on your arm, tattoo it on your forehead, say it in the shower, do whatever is necessary to get this idea in your head. This is going to give you so much power to go and create everything that you want to create.

I can't tell you the last time I used the word *can't* and believed it. Other than in the previous sentence! And I want to encourage you to take that word out of your vocabulary too. You either choose or you don't choose. You either want or you don't want — no more can'ts.

You need to know you're not the only or the first person dealing with issues around what can and can't be done, making all your challenges about you, or worrying about getting things right or getting caught up in worrying about what other people are going to say. You're not the only person stuck with the lack of every distinction we have talked about. You might start to recognise that your clients are getting stuck in these types of areas as well. Therefore, you can apply the appropriate distinction to your clients. Or, like I have done, make up your own distinction from your own insights and experience.

It can be done, and you can do it! From that way of seeing your coaching business, what new actions do you see to take? How do you feel? What thoughts appear? Are they low- or high-vibrational? Unshakeable or shakeable? True or false? Useful or not?

Sobiya's Breakthrough

'I wanted to be a significant thought leader in my field. I wanted to work and collaborate with some of the leading figures in the self-development field.'

Once Sobiya switched her mindset and understood that she wasn't selling herself but was instead serving her clients, she transformed as a coach.

'I was able to distance myself from the concept of "selling", which was superficial, and ground myself in integrity, power, and authenticity. I learned that serving powerfully is all about the client and what is best for them. Coming from this place, I ask them honest, bold, and daring questions that lead to breakthroughs and transformations in my clients.

'I believed that people would judge me for being a woman of colour, from an ethnic minority who wore a hijab (head-scarf), and that would be a big obstacle in my path to success. I wouldn't be able to work with high-performing individuals and create the success, impact, and revenue that I wanted in my coaching business.

'It was in the very first conversation with Ryan where that belief was completely shattered. I gained an insight that changed my life and business forever.'

Through that conversation, Sobiya realised that she is meant to powerfully serve the people who come on her path.

'I can help change and transform their lives. Those who judge me were never meant to be on my path, nor would I ever be able to serve them. In that instance, there was a rock-solid belief that formed which launched me onto an exponential trajectory.'

Sobiya very quickly went on to work with CEOs, managing directors, doctors, and other high-performing individuals. She generated twice the revenue in her first year of her part-time coaching business than she did in her teacher's role.

'The team at HPC has continued to support and guide me even after I graduated from their program. Not only have they been incredible coaches, but I have made lifelong friends with them. I am a full-time coach now — I resigned from my 15-year teaching profession, and I have found my purpose and WHY in the work that I do as a leadership and confidence coach. I am looking to grow and expand my coaching business and employ people to help me do that.

'Through this process, I can connect authentically, shine a light on the challenges my clients are facing, and show them how I can help them as a coach. It is a simple yet powerful way to create a connection, show my magic as a coach, and serve those whom I am speaking to. ... I work with clients who inspire me every time I coach them. They are high achievers and incredible human beings. I receive so much from them in every conversation — it truly is a magical space to hold.'

Sobiya is a leadership and confidence coach. She empowers leaders to create breakthroughs in their confidence so they can lead with clarity, resilience, and purpose.

4
Unshakeable Belief

It all starts with a willingness to believe.

Deb came to us with a belief system that she was an imposter and that at some point she would be found out. She required external validation and therefore was on an emotional roller coaster, feeling successful and confident at one point and then filled with despair and fear at the next.

'In January 2020 I gave notice to my board of directors that I would be retiring from my 30-year career as a childcare director of a multi-site organisation. Then COVID hit, and I was challenged in my role as their leader as never before. I was also offering workshops live and then virtually after March 2020 through my own company. I was excited but unsure of my future and strategies for success with my vision board workshop-focused company. I had taken a coaching program which provided some basics around uncovering my niche and market research but not how to scale as a full-time career coach — I had been averaging $2K–$3K a month. As I left my full-time career in July 2020, I knew that unless I invested in myself and my company, I would be creating the same impact as I had been in the past two years. I felt sick to my stomach as I dipped into my savings to join the program, but I also had a feeling of anticipation as I stepped into the vision I had created only two years before.'

Deb did not have Unshakeable Belief. It was inside of her but inconsistent. She was absolutely willing to have it, though, and it was only a matter of time.

Essential Element 1: Unshakeable Belief

Unshakeable Belief is at the core of building an impactful coaching business. That's why it's the first Essential Element in being a High-Performing Coach.

Up until that moment when I turned thirty, my belief in myself was all kinds of shakeable, and what was worse was that I didn't even know it. Throughout my life, I always had a big ambition and was confident enough to pursue those ambitions. They ranged from being a football player to an actor, a DJ, followed by multiple attempts to become a successful entrepreneur. When I say 'multiple', I mean 20+ tries.

Every single endeavour followed the same path. I would start full of ambition, enthusiasm, and motivation. I would share it with a bunch of people, and everyone would get excited for me. They would be supporting me through whatever it was I was going for. At the start, I would excel, which would give me more confidence and more hope. Then at some point, something wouldn't work out. I would start to experience some failure. Then I would be good for maybe the first two or three failures, but when it came to the fourth failure and beyond, I would start to withdraw myself. I would start to look for excuses to do something else. I would start to believe that I didn't really like this in the first place, or maybe it wasn't the right thing for me. Eventually, I would do a U-turn and find the next big idea and go through the same process.

After that moment I described earlier in East London, when I had a profound personal experience, life was never the same again. As I started to see the truth about my thoughts and the false belief that I wasn't good enough, I was able to move through them as they showed up in my awareness. I began to realise that anytime I was struggling to develop skills, or create results, it just meant I had something to learn. Nothing personal at all. Results don't happen overnight, and skills aren't mastered on the first attempt; they are developed over time. That's what I started to see.

By the time I started really and truly believing in myself, I had a new mission to become a coach. You know what? I failed so much in the first year or two in coaching conversations. Not in them all, but really, I had some horrible moments. I really wasn't getting it 'right' at all! I would project, be right, make wrong, even get defensive in some moments. And rather than getting caught up in guilt, shame, or beliefs that I wasn't good enough or that I would never be good enough, I trusted and knew, without any doubt, that I could become a great coach. I actually still remember a defining moment when this realisation completely dropped — it was a major milestone.

I had just completed a coaching conversation, and it had gone all sorts of sideways. I did feel all the low-vibing feelings. And I said to myself, 'Keep going, one day you'll master this.' Here I was, failing all over the place, and I was actually believing more than ever — this was new, and the moment Unshakeable Belief in myself was born in my awareness, and I have developed it ever since.

It left me wide open to ask for and receive all the help and support that was available to me. It gave me an abundance of energy to do whatever was required of me, and it gave me strength in the days when it was tough. I still had plenty of tough moments in the early days, but now I was able to bounce back! Sometimes it took days, sometimes hours, and then minutes, and then flow. Breakthrough!

This is the kind of outcome Unshakeable Belief can give you too, if you want it.

Let's look a bit deeper into how beliefs work. You've got to imagine that the negative, unconscious beliefs we have are like the puppeteer pulling the strings in the background. We can't always see that they are there. They influence everything that we feel and do and ultimately the results we are experiencing in every aspect of our life. We need to learn how to look behind the curtain and see what's really pulling us.

Conscious Beliefs vs. Unconscious Beliefs

Many of our core beliefs are formed in our unconscious. They have been with us so early and so long that we don't relate to them like a belief, we relate to them like they are the truth. Then we live our life based on those 'truths', and they pile up in the background, out of sight, hidden from us, but they keep shaping our whole experience of life and all of our results.

What's a conscious belief? We seldom slow down to give ourselves a chance to figure that out. We just go based on what we initially believe (think). We've got to cultivate some sense of awareness to see exactly what we're believing, take a breath, slow down, and examine our thoughts to see if they are true, aligned with what we want, or just something we made up that is zapping our energy.

And what's most important beyond the question around what is true or false is the answer to the question: Is this belief (way of thinking) leaving me feeling good, empowered, and aligned with the results my heart desires, or is it leaving me feeling not so good, disempowered, and out of alignment with the results my heart desires?

Boiling it down, the question can turn into: Is this an unconscious belief I am acting out or a conscious belief I am choosing for myself?

Boiling it all the way down, the question can simply become: Is this belief (or thought) useful?

If we're living with false, low-vibrational thinking and acting out a multitude of unconscious beliefs, then we'll create matching results, or we won't create results at all. It's really that simple. If we live from consciously created beliefs, creating more deliberate and intentional thoughts, we will take more effective action and create results that are aligned with these thoughts instead. We will feel free, empowered, and happy. Thinking like this is simply a skill, and like anything else, it's a skill anyone can learn — and even master — if they really want to.

When it comes to your coaching business, I want you to consider the three specific beliefs that are holding you back and getting in your way the most.

#1: Your belief about yourself

You may have some belief about yourself that paralyses you or at least is slowing you down. You might believe that you can't create high-paying clients. You also might believe that you need more training, or you need more accreditations — that otherwise, potential clients won't want to work with you. Ultimately, you might be creating a belief that you're not good enough. This thought is usually at the bottom of your limiting beliefs.

These kinds of thoughts bring about more feelings of anxiety, worry, stress, pressure, fear, doubt, guilt, or shame.

This is space in which you are now relating to yourself.

#2: Your belief about your potential clients

Consider there's something that you may believe about your potential clients that stops you from taking the necessary action to talk to those people, create clients, and build your business. You might have the belief that these potential clients don't want to hear from you. It could be the belief that they aren't willing to pay for your coaching. Maybe you believe that they'll expect you to have all the answers, and you know that you don't. You might be afraid that they see you as an imposter. Ultimately, there may be some kind of belief that they will judge you and find you out!

These kinds of thoughts bring about more feelings of anxiety, worry, stress, pressure, fear, doubt, guilt, or shame.

This is space in which you are now approaching or not approaching your clients.

#3: Your belief about the business that you're building

You might have a false belief about the business you're building. You might believe that you're not able to learn what it takes to build a business. You might believe that you're not the one who's going to create a $5K–$20K per month income (or whatever your goal is). You also might believe that there's too much competition, or there are too many other coaches, especially these days when there's an influx of coaches coming into the industry. You might secretly believe that your business is going to fail! These beliefs, and more, are getting in your way.

These kinds of thoughts bring about more feelings of anxiety, worry, stress, pressure, fear, doubt, guilt, or shame.

This, then, is the space in which you are building the business.

Now, see what resonates for you in everything I've just shared. Take a moment and reflect on that. Stop reading and see if there's something else. What's the belief that you have about your business, your clients, or yourself that's getting in your way?

The Impact of Limiting Beliefs

On your business

You're probably doing busywork because in the background you just don't believe you can do it. Or maybe you then start to believe that you can't replicate the income that you used to make from your previous job. If you believe that, there's going to be a huge emotional impact because you're believing that you can't have what you want. You're believing that you're not going to be financially secure. You're believing that you can't have it all. One belief feeds into another. Then, with these beliefs, we start to create a world for ourselves. This is the world that we end up living in, but we don't even know it. Then we wonder why we don't get the results that we want. This is not what being a High-Performing Coach looks like. However, it is what the journey to becoming one does look like for many of us, so keep reading!

On your potential clients

Next, your beliefs affect how you interact with your potential clients. You're afraid to sound like you're selling them something if you have a conversation with them. That is a horrible impact because you don't want to appear salesy. You certainly don't want anybody to think for a second that you're a salesperson. This is a huge concern that comes up for new coaches, and they get stuck in it.

Let's remember that there is no selling when it comes to coaching. We're not selling; we are serving. That's connected to the distinction in the previous chapter. This idea that you're selling is a false belief that you project onto your clients. When you believe it, it takes you away from your commitment to serving people. Another low-vibrational belief around getting clients is believing that they can't afford it or they won't pay for your services. Now, when you do something like that, what you're doing is you're putting your clients in a tightly sealed box. When you put clients in a box, you end up making decisions about clients, what they can and cannot do, and what they are and are not capable of, which is the opposite of what coaching is all about.

As a coach, we've got to provide a space for our clients to dream bigger than they've ever dreamed before. They need a space to believe that they can create anything they want. Before we've even had a conversation with them, we can't already decide what they can and cannot do, based on our beliefs. We are projecting our beliefs onto our clients. Any belief about your client that's limiting them is the opposite of what coaching is all about. This is not what being a High-Performing Coach looks like.

On yourself

Last, there is your limiting belief about yourself. If you have a belief that you are not able to create high-paying clients, then the impact might be that you're not even trying. If you believe that you can't do something, your brain won't waste any time or energy trying to do it, because it's a very highly effective machine at conserving its energy. You're trying your best, but if you look at your actions and your results, you'll see how these beliefs are impacting you.

Maybe you believe that you're not a good enough coach, or you can't command the high fee. Very often what I see is that people who are in this space keep spinning their wheels. They go around and around for months or maybe years. They enter programs and confront strategies that they never fully apply, because this belief in the background hinders them from making real headway. Often coaches are not creating the results they want to create because they get totally stuck on asking for money. However, the problem isn't ever about asking for money. The problem is always the belief in the background. ALWAYS.

Right now, allow yourself to examine which limiting beliefs exist for you. Maybe it's one or a few of the above, or maybe you have others. How are they impacting you? When you tell yourself, for example, that you are not worthy of a high fee, what tends to happen is that coaches usually work for free or for a very low fee. They'll avoid offering their programs because they don't want to have to confront the money conversation. They project onto their clients that they won't have the money. But really, it's because, deep down, they believe that they're not worthy of asking for it. Then, of course, not asking or not offering your programs means that then you have no business.

All you're doing is coaching for free, and that seems to be fun at the start, but it has a very short shelf life. You can't be satisfied working for free because you've got bills to pay. The truth is, you are worthy. All of these things eventually start coming to the surface. This is a kind of conversation that I hope we can bring to the surface faster for you, so you can start creating the results that you want.

Knowing Is the Booby Prize

As you're reading, you might be thinking that you're aware of how important beliefs are and that you 'know' all this. But are you acting in alignment with this knowledge? Knowing alone doesn't give you anything. Knowing is a fallacy; it is the ego trying to protect itself from confronting the truth about itself. The ego can't handle it if you've got it wrong and maybe you don't have all the answers. Our way of defending ourselves from that kind of reality is to say to ourselves, 'I know'. But the truth is, knowing alone doesn't make any difference, because it's not about what you know, it's about being aware and about what you do with that awareness. If you know that your beliefs are shaping your reality, yet you are not creating results, then the truth is that you're actually acting out unconscious limits in one way or another. The exciting part is the opportunity in all this — you get to deal with it, break through, and create results, and then all that wisdom is yours to give to your clients. How magical is that? And simple! Far from easy, though ...

So, be careful when you say 'I know'. I'm very careful (or a better way to say it would be conscious) when I want to tell somebody I know what they're telling me, because it might well be reinforcing the idea I have about myself that there's something wrong with me. How it shows up is, I've got to convince the world that I already knew the answer. I'm enough — see! If I observe that for myself and I catch myself, then I can let it go before I empower the idea that there's something wrong with me. I'd like you to do the same. Every time you're about to say you know, just watch, because it might be the limiting belief pulling the strings in the background.

This impact and false belief combined are taking you on a particular trajectory. What is this belief? What is this impact and where is this impact taking you? This is what we've got to start to uncover if we want to create Unshakeable Belief. Before we create Unshakeable Belief, we've got to get clear on what beliefs are already there, the subsequent impact of these beliefs, and where they're headed. Why? So we see the truth about what's really going on and we're motivated to do something about it. If we're not motivated to do something about it, we would just keep those old beliefs in place.

Take some time now and get clear about what's being revealed about your unconscious beliefs and habitual thinking.

Creating Unshakeable Belief

How do we create Unshakeable Belief? It's simple. To create Unshakeable Belief, you need to start with a willingness to believe. With a willingness to believe, then everything can start to open up. Once we have a willingness to believe that we are more than capable and absolutely deserving of building the business of our dreams, a willingness to believe that there are clients out there who would love to work with us, that we can build a wildly successful and profitable business, that our coaching can make a difference, that we are good enough, that we are worthy, that we can have the business and life of our dreams ... everything starts to shift.

With a willingness to believe, we can start to imagine what to do next. If you were willing to believe that you were enough, that your coaching was impactful (or that you could learn how it can be impactful), that you're worthy of a high fee, and that you can generate thousands of dollars per client, what actions would you take next? Thoughts start to open up, and the actions you see you need to take start to change. All of a sudden, you might find the right pool of people to talk to about your coaching. All of a sudden, you might be experiencing the desire to show up on social media in a way you've never done before.

Maybe you want to create your first Facebook Live. Maybe you get yourself to that critical point that I did and all the other success stories I'll share with you in this book, like hire an expert and be willing to invest — with a willingness to believe you'll make all your money back and then some! This kind of willingness to believe makes action — and the right action — natural and effortless. Without it, life is confusing, often terrifying; business is hard work, things don't come easy, and we don't know why. And yet, it was within you all along, you just didn't believe it or struggled to keep believing no matter what. Perhaps the scared you has been holding yourself back from the bold you that you can now create for yourself through a willingness to believe and a commitment to having Unshakeable Belief.

When you believe in yourself, new openings for action start to show up as you open yourself up through this willingness. However, not all of these actions are necessarily the most useful steps. You've got to highlight the most effective actions. Start with the first five or so. The next step is to take those actions and keep repeating the process. That is how you create Unshakeable Belief. I'm never surprised at the profound breakthrough results that can happen when we are willing to believe in ourselves and willing to act in alignment with that belief. When you act, the universe has your back. The universe provides, responds, and feeds those people who are open and who are willing to go and create.

If you were willing to believe that you were a good enough coach and could build what you wanted to build, maybe you would decide that you're going to follow this book's processes. From there, you discover the real difference that you can make. Maybe you'll start to find clients. You will start connecting with people who are facing the kind of challenges that you're good at solving. You will start feeling confident enough to offer your programs. Surprise, surprise: a bunch of people will say yes, a bunch of people will say no, and a bunch of people will be in the middle, and you get the chance to learn how to empower them to a clear no or yes! All of a sudden, this willingness to believe, started as a seed, begins to grow. That willingness to believe will create paying clients and build your confidence as you become a better coach, a better entrepreneur, and better at building a successful business. All of that starts with just the willingness to believe.

All I had at the beginning of my journey was the willingness to believe. Every morning in the shower I would say, 'I'm good enough. I'm good enough. I'm good enough. I can do this. You got this, Ryan!' All variations of that. I looked crazy talking to myself, but I knew that after speaking negatively and unconsciously to myself for years, I needed to build a new muscle!

At the same time, I was taking a whole bunch of actions, and I was getting better at what I was doing. Now I was finding evidence that I could do this, which fed my belief, and I found ways to take smarter and more effective actions. I would get better and create more results, and then the vicious circle started to turn around to a very positive upward spiral, and it's never stopped since. I was going beyond anywhere I'd ever been before, and so can you.

In 2017, when I needed to invest $20K to learn what I needed to learn to create high-fee clients, I didn't have that kind of money, remember? All I did have was Unshakeable Belief, and everything flowed from there.

Would you like to be able to:

- Find the courage to invest? Start with a willingness to believe.

- Find the courage to borrow? Willingness to believe.

- Find the courage to take massive action? Willingness to believe.

- Face one failure after another? Willingness to believe.

- Deal with yourself and get straight in the mirror? Willingness to believe.

- Hold your hands up and ask for help? Willingness to believe.

- Invite potential clients to have a powerful experience? Willingness to believe.

- Offer your high-fee programs? Willingness to believe.

The outcome? More and more Unshakeable Belief.

I think you get the point ...

Plenty of new coaches come up against the idea that they aren't good enough when it comes time to spending money on their training, although many don't realise it's just a belief running in the background. Since they don't believe they're good enough, they convince themselves that they don't have the money. But the truth is, they do have the money; they could find it. They just don't believe that it's all going to work out. They talk themselves out of it, and then they end up living in that world until they have a realisation all on their own — or somebody like me shows up and helps them have a breakthrough. Or not.

This is exactly what many of your clients are doing too, and what they are also dealing with, and it's all the more reason why you must break through it first. Otherwise, you won't be able to help them because you're stuck on the same thing.

'Yes, I know all that, and I really believe it, but ...'

It's right there ...

Can you see it?

Can you feel it?

Can you smell it!?

BE AWARE OF THE 'BUT'.

Are you beginning to recognise those moments when you talk yourself away from, and out of alignment with, who you really are and what you're out to accomplish? That's the unconscious running the show.

And then we wonder why we feel tired, heavy, frightened …

And we wonder why we're not creating results …

If you want to soar in your coaching business and learn what it really takes to help your clients soar too, you must cultivate, integrate, and generate a more conscious and deliberate way of thinking and talking …

It's all in your speaking. It's right there …

'I hear you, Ryan, but …'

That is not Unshakeable Belief. That is your head talking. Can you hear it?

Trust you can create what you want, and it can give you the permission to speak it out boldly and unapologetically.

Get deliberate and intentional around how you talk to yourself about yourself, how you talk to yourself about your clients and your business, how you talk to others about yourself, and how you talk to the world about what you are up to. Oh, and stay humble while you do.

This Is Unshakeable Belief

As the saying goes, 'Be careful what you wish for!' I say, 'Be careful what you believe in!'

Your belief creates your reality. You are choosing what you believe, moment to moment, with the thoughts you are having and the things you are saying. So, be mindful about what you think and say, because your thinking and speaking create worlds.

What would happen if you adopted the belief that your business, with time and commitment, will become a business that makes a real difference in the world?

What would happen if you adopted the belief that your business could enable you to have the life you really want and be an inspiration for others so that they can have the life they want too?

What would happen if you adopted the belief that your clients might be grateful that you connected with them?

What would happen if you adopted the belief that your clients can be, do, and have whatever they truly want in their businesses and their lives?

What would happen if you adopted the belief that you have everything you need right now to go out there and powerfully serve people?

What would happen if you adopted the belief that you can be, do, and have whatever you truly want in your business and in your life?

Here's a fun one: What would happen if you were willing to believe that you could build a business that left you feeling great; that was structured so you could live anywhere on the planet with WiFi; that made more than enough money for you to have the lifestyle of your dreams; and that allowed you to work around 15 to 20 hours per week? That's what I was willing to believe a few years back, and guess what? It happened! This is not bragging; this is a testament.

These are just some of the very same beliefs I generated and have continued to believe which helped me build multiple high-fee, six- and seven-figure coaching businesses, and that enabled me to help thousands of coaches all over the world create incredible results in their business too.

You might feel resistance here. You might not find it easy to believe such things. This may also be a function of a lack of permission. So, try giving yourself the permission to be the kind of human being who can be, do, have whatever you want.

Could you give yourself the permission to speak it out boldly and unapologetically? If you connect with your heart right now, you'll see that your heart is completely aligned with these ideas and is saying yes, yes, yes!

Try it right now: put your hand on your heart, close your eyes, and get profoundly connected to its wisdom. What is it telling you?

And this is what it looks like when I talk about Unshakeable Belief and building your business from the heart.

It's painfully simple and, for most coaches, the hardest thing to do.

And yet, with practice, like riding a bike, it can become an easy, effortless, and absolutely thrilling ride.

Then What?

To create extraordinary results, we simply need an extraordinary belief structure and a tried, tested, and effective set of actions.

To make the shift from 'willing to' to 'unshakeable' requires actions that are in alignment with that belief …

When we are in action, we begin to reveal the truth, and those old beliefs get busted because we get to see what's real.

> 'I'm so happy you reached out!'
> The belief that no one wants to hear from you
> — busted.

> 'I'd love to have a call with you — sounds great!'
> The belief that no one is going to be open to having your help — busted.

'How can I work with you?'
The belief that no one would want to work with you — busted.

'How can I pay you?'
The belief that no one will pay you a high fee — busted.

'I have a friend whom I'd love to tell about you and your work. Do you have any space for new clients?'
The belief that this is not going to work — busted.

'My first $10K/$20K month!'

The belief that it can't be done — busted.

And what starts to get really interesting is that after your first $10K/$20K month, you start seeing really clearly who you are and what you can accomplish — limitless.

We'll go deeper into the actions that are most effective to make these results happen in the upcoming chapters as we continue to dive deep into the Essential Elements.

Deb's Breakthrough

By uncovering and clearing her limiting beliefs, Deb found within herself the freedom to be confidently vulnerable.

'When I reveal my personal story, I provide space for my clients to feel safe to do so as well. When we are able to be the "Real Deal", as Ryan would say — we are empowered and are unstoppable.'

Deb initially identified herself as a workshop facilitator and therefore felt limited in impact and earning potential. By creating a one-to-one and group high-fee program, she tripled her monthly revenue. 'My program is now global, being online versus exclusively in-person Canadian workshops. The expertise to leverage social media platforms such as LinkedIn and Facebook groups has been valuable to attract clients.

'Prior to HPC, I did not know how to consistently attract clients. The protocols and scripts are valuable because they work. When I stopped trying to do it on my own and followed the HPC proven methods, I was able to create high-paying clients and offer my clients powerful breakthroughs. I began to view training and coaching calls not from the lens of a client but as a coach. All HPC coaches model meaningful questions as they lean in to coach new or existing clients.'

The ongoing workshops, open coaching sessions, Facebook group, and accountability group have been instrumental in growing her business after she graduated from the program. As her company levels up, having the support and resources of the HPC community has been invaluable and has contributed to its success.

'My income is well over $20K/month, with paid workshops and high-paying clients. I have served 175 clients since starting the HPC program. I am an empowered, confident personal development coach. I have unshakeable belief in myself, my clients, and in my business.'

Exercise:
New Beliefs

- What new beliefs about your coaching business are you now creating that are aligned with the vision, mission, values, and desired results you imagined for yourself in Chapter 2?

- What new beliefs about your potential clients are you now creating that are aligned with vision, mission, values, and desired results you imagined for yourself in Chapter 2?

- What new beliefs about yourself are you now creating that are aligned with vision, mission, values, and desired results you imagined for yourself in Chapter 2?

Go to www.ryanmathie.com/book and access my Unshakeable Belief training. This is the original training that I designed and have shared with thousands of coaches all over the world, which gave them a direct access to Unshakeable Belief for themselves and their clients.

5
Business Foundations

Building the plane on the way up.

Manj was juggling his job at investment bank J.P. Morgan with building his coaching business, charging clients around £50–£100 per one-off session or a block of four.

'I heard about HPC through a friend who had worked with Ryan and the team,' Manj says. 'She told me she went from charging a low fee per hour to now charging £2K for a program, and I called BS on that because I knew there was no way you could charge that kind of money for coaching. There was simply no way a human being is charging this kind of money for coaching.'

The foundations of Manj's business were rudimentary. He had a popular blog and was creating clients, albeit exchanging time for money. He was doing well by most coaches' standards, generating around £2K per month.

However, it wasn't sustainable, nor was it going to grow, until he experienced a shift in his beliefs and implemented more effective Business Foundations.

Essential Element 2: Business Foundations

To build something great and long-lasting requires intelligent design, rigorous testing, and continuous development. And that doesn't mean we need to take all day about it. It's simpler than that and can move with speed.

We are laying our foundations using our best thinking, from the understanding that the more we experience, test, and verify, the more solid our foundations can become, while at the same time we can begin to create clients, make an impact, and get cash flowing in our business. In that process, we develop our foundations, lay them deeper, and make them stronger, and on and on it goes.

There are four key aspects to the Business Foundations.

Niche

Your niche is the group of prospective clients you serve, the specific problem that you help them solve, and a particular set of results that you help them achieve. You need to be clear about the people you're helping, the problem you're solving, and what they really want.

Messaging

Your messaging is a statement summarising the above in a way so that when that group of people hear it, they know you can help them achieve the results they're looking for.

Method (Or Process)

Your unique method or process is the way in which you actually help that group of people solve that particular problem to attain the desired result.

High-Fee Program

Your high-fee program is where you deliver your process and the environment (or space) you create to help clients achieve optimal results.

The technical business set-up is a critical part of your foundations and simpler than you'd think during launch phase. For reasons I hope will be obvious, we won't be covering the technical aspect of foundations in this book. With that being said, I'd like to clarify that all you *really* need to get started — from a practical/tools perspective — is a way to take payments and a way to schedule calls. That's it!

What's Your Niche?

Shortly, we'll do some work in this book around discovering your niche, but first I want to share some important wisdom that will support your process whether you are able to discover your niche, right here and now, or not.

A niche can sometimes be confusing. Most new coaches get stuck here. They'll all be told that to find their way, they need a niche from the get-go. That works for some and keeps many others stuck because most coaches don't understand it and they're simply not ready to discover it.

When I started out, I was told I needed a niche, and I didn't understand what it was. I was even more confused after I Googled it. Even after going through a multitude of support and coaching processes to find it, it wasn't clear to me. I didn't want to waste time in serving clients and generating revenue, so instead of going down a rabbit hole, I simply let go of the idea of a niche. I sensed it wasn't flowing, so instead I started working with anyone I believed I could help. I was still able to create five-figure months and a very successful coaching business.

I'm sharing this because I want you to know that to get started, you don't need a niche either — although it is certainly ideal, preferred, and where you want to settle eventually. Of the coaches we've helped, the ones who had the biggest results had a clearly defined niche or discovered their niche earlier in the process. But it's not compulsory to get started and to create impact and high-paying clients.

Sometimes your niche is not ready to be discovered, because you need more time and experience. You may need to explore all the different avenues of helping different groups of people. If that's the case, trust that. Discovering your niche, like anything in life, happens when it's the right time. It could be weeks, months, or a couple of years.

Sometimes niches are only right for a certain period in your career. Two years later, a new niche might emerge as you keep evolving, your ideas change, and you get to a different level within yourself. Your niche isn't necessarily for life. At the same time, it could be. Time will tell.

If you do have a clear niche, great. This is where you ideally want to be.

If you don't have one, you can definitely still build a great business and trust that you will discover it along the way. This is great because it's another thing that doesn't need to stop you, and you can create revenue, refine your coaching skills, have a blast, and build your business all at the same time. I'm committed to the belief that nothing needs to ever stop me, and I want you to get committed to that too.

Follow the Flow

If you know you have no idea what your niche is, then you want to see yourself more as a general life coach. There are many exciting and creative ways you can express this: Transformational Coach, Empowerment Coach, Breakthrough Coach, or Mindset Coach, for example — as a coach who can help people in multiple areas. The best way to figure out your niche is to talk to people and start coaching clients.

My opinion is that it's a good idea to always go wider at the start than to go too narrow. I see too many coaches cut so many people out at the start. Then their options are limited, and they don't have enough momentum to sustain their business or figure anything out given that so much gets clear while coaching and working with clients in the first place.

When you're unsure of your niche, go wider, and as you go through the process of talking to people, coaching, and serving, you start to see patterns and who you're drawn to. Your niche will present itself to you soon enough. Hold on. Trust the process and your intuition.

And remember, the fact you can create revenue while figuring this out is of great benefit.

To give you an example, I was working with many kinds of clients — on relationships, health, their business, their personal life, and so on ... then all of a sudden, a flow of clients showed up for me who were coaches struggling with a lack of confidence. I started to connect with other coaches more. Before I knew it, I was training a lot of coaches in Unshakeable Belief and how to go deeper in their coaching.

At the end of the process, when I asked, 'What's next?', almost every coach would tell me they were broke and didn't know how to start their own business. After hearing that three or four times, I saw that this group didn't just need help with Unshakeable Belief and coaching skills, they needed to know how to create clients and build their business — and I could show them all three. That's when the penny dropped. My niche was to help coaches build their business. That's an evolution that took place over two years.

For me, it was all about trusting the flow. Do this, and you'll find your niche. You allow yourself to go with the flow so you can keep serving people, master your craft, and build your business. Be open to what is flowing towards you rather than resisting and trying to make something else happen that isn't showing up. I often see coaches who miss the wood for the trees regarding this; they tell me their niche is 'X', and when I poke and prod around, I help them realise that what's flowing towards them is 'Y' or 'Z'.

Discover Your Niche

In terms of discovering your niche, I suggest you think from a few key places. Think about the big breakthroughs you've had in your life. What were they? Other things to consider:

- What are some of the things you've had more success in?

- What is your magic? What are your skillsets?

- What do you feel passionate about?

- What are you truly great at?

- Who is already flowing to you?

- Who is already in your network? How can you help this group the most?

For example, I left job after job, tried over and over again during the pursuit of a more fulfilling career. I was on a mission to discover my purpose and I went through it all — from leaving jobs with no money and nowhere to go, only an insatiable hunger to figure it all out, to creating startups with some success, only to discover along the way 'this is not it', and moving on, trusting my gut. I've gone through that process to discover my purpose and discovered it, and I know what it's like, what it takes, and how to handle all that fear and uncertainty. I could write a book on the art of going for what you want and letting nothing get in your way!

Another very personal story is a transformation and major breakthrough in my life ... my relationship with my dad, James.

For almost twenty years, my dad and I didn't speak. Mine was a challenging upbringing, to say the least. Dad was a very lost and angry soul who wasn't ready for the responsibilities of parenthood, and there was violence. I held a lot of resentment towards him for so long and blamed him for everything that happened back then.

I was, and still am, very protective of my mum, Morag, who I have always been very close to, so I became fierce towards him in a silent and dismissive way. For so many years, I never thought about my dad, never spoke about him, and acted like he never existed.

When I started on my path, he was one of the first people who came to my mind. I began a slow process of letting go and forgiving him. One day in 2011, in a coaching conversation, I had a life-changing breakthrough I'll never forget ... *I realised I'd made up a story about him that he was a monster.*

Right away, I saw he was not a monster.

He was just dealing with what he was dealing with, and, without justifying his mistakes, I could see he'd done his best.

My next thoughts were, 'Well, if he's not a monster, maybe I could like him. If I could like him, maybe I could love him.' Even as I write this, so many years later, my emotions stir ...

I ran out of the room I was in and called my brother Jason to get my dad's number, as I didn't even have that much. I was in a flood of tears at what I was getting in touch with: my sadness, grief, compassion, and love ...

With a lump in my throat, I dialled Dad's number.

It went to voicemail, so I said, 'Dad, it's Ryan. You probably didn't expect to hear from me today, but I'm calling to tell you I love you and that I'm sorry for blaming you. It's all going to be OK now. I just want my dad back.'

This was the first time I ever felt love for my dad, and it was the first time I ever told him. Next time I looked at my phone, there were seven missed calls and two voice notes. We had a very emotional call that day — all was forgiven, the past was back in the past where it belonged, and we were present with each other and extremely close from that moment on.

In early 2021, Dad was diagnosed with terminal cancer.

It was aggressive, and one Saturday in August, he slipped into a coma. I was out of the country and began running a race against the clock which got me to his bedside at the hospice on the Wednesday at 5:30 pm.

All Dad could do was breathe.

For the previous four days, his eyes had been fixed wide open, totally non-responsive, but I knew he could hear me.

I told him about all the posts of prayer and love from social media, people he'd known, and many whom he'd never known but who had offered their support.

I thanked him for waiting for me to get back to his bedside, for giving me life, and made sure he knew I admired how he handled his painful battle of repeated illness like a soldier.

Mostly, we sat together in silence, just being together. Touching his face, holding his hands, rubbing his arms and shoulders, kissing his head. Dad and I had said it all many a time before — we were at peace and complete with each other.

Around 7:30 pm I had a strong urge to do something I'd always wanted to do with him — meditate together — and knew I would not get another chance.

I told him the intention of our meditation was for him to know he was loved, to know he was forgiven, and to know he was not alone.

It was a deeply spiritual experience. Dad's breathing became deeper and more intense throughout, and then it gradually trailed off and I just knew he was going to leave at any moment.

I let him know it was OK, he was OK, everything would be OK. He could go now if he was ready.

I watched as he breathed shorter and shorter until he took his last and went on to whatever awaited him on the other side.

He died in my hands at 8:25 pm, having waited for me to come home, some four hours after I got to him.

My eldest brother, Darrin, Dad's main carer, arrived a few moments after. It was a very emotional experience — even beautiful and magical — that we got to share together.

Writing this now, I feel a deep sadness and grief, as well as immense love and gratitude. And I wanted to share it in absolute honour of coaching. Without it, this beautiful ending simply would not have been possible for me and my dad.

Helping other people heal their childhood wounds and reunite them with their fathers, or helping people get complete with their parents or family challenges is an area that is very important to me and could have been another and very rewarding area for me to niche into. Gratefully, I have found a way to be able to help coaches with these topics too when we continue on a deeper journey, working together.

What about for you?

When it comes time to discovering your niche, you want to look from those deep and rich places: your breakthroughs, defining moments, passions, experiences, skillsets, and what you would love to do more of and feel called to. In that process, you might start to see something more clearly, and your niche may emerge.

You'll know it when you find it. It's bigger than just your niche. It's your mission. Your life's purpose.

A great niche lights up your heart AND it also makes practical business sense too. See if you can find a niche that is balanced between heart and mind. If you want to help the unemployed, it's going to come with its obvious challenges. It's not impossible! However, you might want to think about another more suitable niche for a high-fee business if that's what you want, and then when your business is thriving, you'll be better equipped to serve those groups of people less suitable for high-fee.

If nothing is emerging, you can make a decision not to make a decision and apply the approach mentioned earlier, working with anyone you believe you can help and want to work with, trusting it will come when it's ready.

Narrow Niche Messaging

If you have a great niche, we can focus on specific messaging for that niche.

Messaging is about being clear in what you do. Your website and social media profiles should be crystal clear about who you help and how you help them. Sounds obvious, but you'd be amazed at how many coaches miss something here. Either they don't say anything or what they say tries so hard to sound good and be clever that nobody knows what they do. **Your messaging should always be clear, NEVER clever.**

Be consistent across all your platforms. Understand that your audience will stalk you — and you should welcome the idea of becoming a public figure! They're looking for evidence they can trust you and believe in you. They're looking for evidence you're the right person to help them. SO, make their life easy by being consistent online with your messaging and authentic in your being. Otherwise, people will lose faith in you and move on to someone else.

Here's how you figure your messaging out.

For this particular exercise, you do actually require a niche! If you don't have yours yet, come back and try this when you do. Or it might help you along in the process ...

Imagine you have a hundred people who fit within your niche in a room right now. If you asked every person in the room what their biggest challenge was, what do you think they would say?

For example, if your niche is leaders, you ask the question, and from your own unique experience and knowledge of leaders, you get in touch with the answer.

Now let's do another ... Same set-up again, but this time the question is: 'What do you really want?' Again, from your unique experience and knowledge, get in touch with your answer. What do you imagine they would all agree on?

Now you have your group of people, what they are being challenged by, and what they really want.

And if you work with leaders, for example, here are a few ways you might express your messaging (often referred to as an elevator pitch, although I never use this or liked this term):

1. Supporting leaders achieve greater success by leading from the heart

2. Helping anxious and overwhelmed leaders turn breakdowns into breakthroughs

3. Helping CEOs and leaders strategise their careers and lead with clarity, confidence, and purpose

4. Helping leaders be more effective by creating more balance in their lives

Whatever you create now is simply your best starting point. For example, if leaders are your niche, move in that direction and, as you talk to leaders, ask them the same questions you just asked yourself and note the responses. They'll either validate your ideas or feed you new ones, and with each and every conversation you will refine and dial in your messaging.

Take your messaging and put it straight onto LinkedIn, Facebook, Instagram, everywhere your clients are, and all the places you are sharing your gold, in as clear and simple terms as possible. Make it about your audience and their problems and desired outcomes. What speaks to people most is when you can cut straight to what they want. People want what they want, so make sure you're speaking clearly about those big, inspiring, and deeply desired outcomes.

Ultimately, there's no right or wrong answer here. You'll probably tweak your messaging a hundred times over, but you have to use your best thinking at the start, then go from there and move on.

For more inspiration and ideas, go and research other experts in your niche. Consume their content, learn from their socials, visit their site, and allow yourself to be fed with inspiration and clarity.

Go to www.ryanmathie.com/book and access my training on discovering your niche.

How Do I Put My Program Together?

Let's get one thing clear: Your program does not have to be the Sistine Chapel. Too many coaches get stuck on the notion that their program needs to be all-singing and all-dancing, with every bell and whistle perfect before they can get started. Not true.

Today, HPC's program is advanced. We have a team of experts, training platforms, videos, email support, and groups that take in everything from support and training to accountability. We didn't start there, though. We only have these things because we're a scaled business that's been developed over time.

Building the plane on the way up!

This is the HPC way, and it's why we and our clients are thriving.

We understand that we have enough to develop something that allows us to get started and trust in the difference that this will make.

And we evolve, edit, improve, remove, and build with time and experience.

I remember a call I had with a potential client back in the early days. He shared proudly about his program and how amazing it was. It sounded great to me, and you know me — I could tell there was more to this story, so I kept digging.

> Me: How long have you been building?
>
> Coach: Two years now ...
>
> Me: How many clients have you created in that time?
>
> Coach: Zero.
>
> Me: How are your finances?
>
> Coach: I'm broke and can hardly sleep at night.

If only he had the distinction Messy vs. Right, right? Right.

Had he been willing to start creating clients when he had a clear enough sense of his program, he could have started taking people through the process, developing the whole experience, making it better, gaining confidence within himself, and creating impact, success stories, and of course, cash.

I'm sharing this to help you realise you don't need much to get something moving and make an impact. Your clients actually get so much value just by having your time — coaching conversations and accountability are where the real power is. It doesn't have to be complicated in the beginning. A little structure will do.

To hammer this point home, when I started my coaching business, all I had was my coaching conversations delivered inside a clearly defined delivery model: a little structure at the start of the journey where we worked on vision, Unshakeable Belief, mindset, and strategy and a little at the end when we explored how far my client had come and what was next. Every other call, I met my clients where they were at. They were powerfully served, each and every time.

What's the name of your program?

To create a program, I love starting with the name first — this will fuel your fire and get you inspired to get it created and out there; if it doesn't leave you wanting to tell people about it, then you haven't got the name right yet.

Then, you must create a clear and powerful method (or process). Again, this can be simple; it just needs to be defined either way. You want to start by thinking about your clients' problems. Beside each problem, write down the impact of that problem, then write down your unique solution.

Next to your unique solution, write down the tools you have to solve that problem. From there, write down the outcomes that are possible from having applied and integrated all that.

The following exercise will help you get clear about what your clients are going through and how you solve it. Try to express your solution in just a few words. Your top three, four, or five solutions are what you extract and what become your process. You can have six or seven if you choose — it's up to you — but in this case, I'd say less is more.

Let me talk you through some of my own examples and thought processes around how I created the first two of the Five Essential Elements, so you can better understand how to do this for yourself.

One of the dominant problems I could see for coaches was their lack of belief in themselves. The impact of that is, they get stuck and don't take effective actions. They don't take risks because they don't believe it will work.

My unique solution is to develop them in Unshakeable Belief.

One of the tools is to go through my Unshakeable Belief training process, another is coaching around their beliefs, and another is applying a set strategy so they can face their limits, create results, and develop Unshakeable Belief in the process. The outcome? Unstoppable.

The second dominant problem is that coaches don't know the most effective ways to set up, set out, and structure their business. They get stuck before they try to offer the programs, or they won't launch them because it's not clear what they're launching anyway.

The solution is their Business Foundations. The tool is to take them through my training and development to help discover their niche, find their messaging, create their program, and establish their fees. When this is all clear and created, the outcome is that coaches are left free, empowered, and confident to go and do the next part — create high-paying clients!

Below is an example of how you extract your process. You look at the problem, the impact, your unique solution, and what tools you will use to fulfil it. Then you extract those solutions and make them your process.

Here's a quick summary of our process:

a. Problem: Limiting belief structure

b. Solution: Unshakeable Belief

c. Outcome: Unstoppable in your life, more powerful in your coaching

a. Problem: No niche, confused messaging, low- or no-fee coaching sessions/packages

b. Solution: Business Foundations

c. Outcome: Confident, set up to win, and highly motivated to get your business moving!

a. Problem: Can't find clients/don't have clients/don't understand how to create high-fee clients

b. Solution: Breakthrough Process

c. Outcome: Ready, willing, and able to cause breakthroughs and create high-fee clients!

a. Problem: Lack of online strategy, confronted by going public

b. Solution: Online Influence

c. Outcome: Growing in confidence, building your network, and attracting clients!

a. Problem: Isolated, alone, learning from peers who are also struggling

b. Solution: Accountability & Coaching

c. Outcome: Inspired and supported by a community, trained and developed by experts; better coach, better entrepreneur, better human being

We need to dig much deeper to really pull out our unique process. However, these problem/solution pairs will get you thinking along the right lines. Take some time now and brainstorm the main problems you see and your process for solving them. The last thing you need to do is to create a name for your unique method that really speaks to you, like the Five Essential Elements speaks to me. You want a name that inspires you and that captures the imagination.

Go to www.ryanmathie.com/book and access my training on creating and designing your very own unique methodology.

Delivery

Again, keep it simple, and keep in mind you can create the delivery of your program, exactly as you wish. The best place to start is to draw upon two things here: your experience and your preferences.

What programs have you been part of? What did you like more/like less about how they were delivered?

What do you want to do, and what don't you want to do?

For example, schedule session times when it works for you. It's important you can look forward to them. I almost never coach on Fridays, and absolutely never on Saturdays or Sundays unless it's a major event.

How many sessions per month? At HPC, we usually run three major sessions per month in our programs, leaving the final week for all of us, clients included, to have space from calls to focus on whatever else we want to focus on. Or you can run sessions with your clients each and every week — you choose.

How long is your program?

- Maybe you want it to be short and punchy over 6, 7, 8, or 9 weeks?

- Maybe you prefer a 3- or 4-month deeper dive?

- Maybe you want to really go the distance with your clients over 6, 9, or 12 months?

You get to make it all up in such a way that it sounds, feels, and looks great for you, and for your clients too!

When I started coaching, I worked with clients over three sessions a month for six months. After four months, it got a little bit repetitive and the energy shifted, so I pivoted from six months to eight weeks and kept my fees the same. This small tweak gave my clients a more focused objective because the finish line was immediately in sight.

A shorter program created a different intentionality for coach and client, producing incredible results. After eight weeks, we talked about where we would go from there, and off we went.

My point is that there's no right or wrong answer. There is wisdom based on experience, and you get to play, create, enjoy, and make it all up.

How do you deliver your process?

- Are you using Google Chat?
- Meeting in person?

If you like in-person meetings, feel free to keep going with it as it fits, but with a global pool of potential clients, you can open yourself up to online, offline — it really doesn't matter; do what works and bear in mind that the main thing is the coaching commitment and process. All you really need is to be able to talk to that person! I have received and given some of the most powerful breakthroughs via a phone call. The power is in the coaching conversation, so make that the priority and deliver it in the best way possible without being rigid.

What support system do you have for between calls, if any?

You might have a Facebook community ... training videos ... email or WhatsApp support ... You might have Voxer as a way of having support between conversations.

Imagine a program you would love to be a part of. How would that be delivered? There's no right or wrong answer. Create it exactly as you like.

Why the High Fee?

I say that anywhere in the region of $1500/$2500 is the entry level to high-fee. There are two reasons we want high fees instead of low fees.

Low-fee coaching is a different type of business. As a new coach, you might be thinking about offering single sessions or a 'value pack' of sessions. But what would you rather be part of as a client? A transformational program or a block of ten?

Right there is an important distinction. We want to inspire our clients, to have them believing they are on the cusp of something life-changing. This is one of the reasons you want a high-fee program. Straight away, the program is optimised for client results because there's a huge commitment to be part of something bigger, something that calls them to rise, and there's a matching commitment to taking action and creating results.

Doing this session by session simply doesn't work in the same way, and we lose a valuable opportunity to start with a bang — a commitment — and build on top of that. With high-fee, the level of commitment, engagement, and value feels different; your clients go to bed excited and can't wait to get into this program because it sounds so good! Offer a low-fee program, and what you're really offering is a low-value program for those who don't want to or are not ready to jump very high. Again, this is OK if that's where you are in your own process. You could even start there and take your low-fee clients on a journey that eventually offers them high-fee. Or build high-fee first, then circle back and create low-fee digital products (my preferred option, as you can create more impact and cash with high-fee, and let people follow the journey toward your high-fee). Either way, being an HPC is about raising the bar for ourselves and our clients and empowering our clients to jump way over it. This is High-Performing Coaching, and your clients will love you for it.

Ask yourself:

- Who do you think is most inspired and ready to take massive action?
  - The client in the transformational program or the client in the block of ten?
- Who do you think has had the biggest breakthrough from the start?
  - The client committing to a low-fee session-by-session agreement or the client who found it within themselves to commit and invest a high fee?
- Who is more likely to show up, do the work, and take more action?
  - The client in a low-level commitment or in a high-fee commitment?
- Who do you think will likely create the most results?
  - The client in a low-level commitment or in a high-fee commitment?
- Which kind of clients do you want to work with?
  - The low-fee, low-committal clients or the high-fee, high-committal clients?
- What kind of coach do you want to be?
  - A coach who has a low barrier to entry or a High-Performing Coach?

- Which coach do you think is likely to build a more thriving business?
  - The low-fee, low-committal coach or the High-Performing Coach?

I trust you now have your own answer to the question, 'Why the high fee?'

The challenge you might encounter

Perhaps the idea of high fees isn't sitting right with you, or you're experiencing some resistance. Why? This is simply because of the conversation you are having with yourself about:

Your clients: 'They won't pay such an amount', 'They'll think I'm trying to rip them off', or 'They'll just find a cheaper coach'.

Your business: 'It's not possible to charge these kinds of numbers for coaching', 'If I set my fees so high, the business won't work', or 'There's no way you can build a coaching business at these kinds of rates'.

Yourself: 'I couldn't charge this amount; it's not right or fair', 'What if I don't deliver?', 'My coaching isn't worth a high fee', or 'I don't want to be greedy'.

By now, you might be starting to see these conversations for what they are: all made up. These thoughts, views, opinions, and beliefs are usually based on your past experiences, what you believe about money, what you believe about your value, what you believe you are worth, and what you believe about what's possible.

The question is, are they true or just what you are telling yourself is true?

With this kind of thought process in place, you will feel conflicted, because deep down you sense that such ideas are limiting you, but while you are stuck inside these thought processes, you can be left confused and often overwhelmed with guilt and even shame.

From your commitment to developing Unshakeable Belief and bringing about a more deliberate and intentional way of creating your own reality through your thinking and speaking, we can shift these limits and bring about a shift inside of you that will free you up to stand taller for your clients, your business, and yourself.

Here are new ways you can start to speak to yourself about your fees:

- 'My clients are big people who deserve the best in life, and they are worth such a meaningful investment in the things they want. With this level of commitment, they can become the kind of person they need to become to create the results they want to create!'

- 'My business is a stand for what can be accomplished by showing people who they are and what they are worth. Building from this kind of energy will create all the impact and financial rewards they could ever dream about!'

- 'Based on all I have been through, taken on, and invested, and the difference I can make to my clients,

I am worth a high fee. And this worthiness is what I can pass on to every one of my clients!'

How do these conversations sound to you? How do they feel? What new way do you now want to start speaking to yourself about your fees that is aligned with who you are and what you are out to accomplish?

Setting your high fee

Now you are ready to set your fees. They should feel exciting and a little edgy; most of all they should feel right for you. Bear in mind that your fees are yours and yours alone; you can set them out as one number today and change them tomorrow and any time you feel the need.

Here's an example of how I helped a client find their fees in 35 seconds, after they had been struggling to set their fees for eight months. I simply asked them to trust the process and answer with a yes or a no. This is literally how it went:

Me: Are your fees $10K?

Coach: No way.

Me: $1K ...

Coach: Nope.

Me: $5K ...

Coach: Hmm, no.

Me: $2.5K?

Coach: Mmmmm, maybe, no.

Me: $3K?

Coach: Yes. That feels really good to me, actually. My fees are $3K.

With experience and success, how you view your fees will start to evolve and change, and all you have to do is trust in that process. Give yourself permission to set your fees in such a way that they feel really good for you — and then own them.

Go to www.ryanmathie.com/book and access my training on creating and designing your very own high-fee program.

Manj's Breakthrough

'I also found it harder to create transformation in people who were taking things session by session. I didn't have a program, so would dart around a lot in my own work, and I never felt like I knew where the next client was coming from. When I created my high-fee program, I quickly signed my first high-paying client at $2K, and I was bricking it! Now I had to deliver ... but I kept Unshakeable Belief in mind and continued to show up. I then charged $3K, $4K, and $4,500! It was confronting, but I began to realise it doesn't mean anything — it's just a number I get to make up that feels good to me!'

Currently, at time of publishing, Manj is averaging £7.5K a month and growing more and more as a coach and entrepreneur.

'I try to stay under twenty clients because of the time commitment vs. other things I want to achieve (training for a quadrathlon) and publishing my book.'

Next, we're helping Manj create a group coaching offer to help take his business and his impact to the next level.

As a Transformation and Relationship Coach, Manj helps people unlock their potential through his program Inner Mastery, so they can live the life they want, instead of merely tolerating the one they have.

Exercise:
Your Business Foundations

- Who do you help and how do you help them? (Niche & Messaging)

- What is the name of your high-fee program?

- What is your new unique process?

- What are your new fees?

- What new beliefs are you starting to form around your earning potential in building your coaching business?

6
Breakthrough Process,
Part I: Connect and Invite

Lead great conversations that are intentional,
meaningful, and grounded in your heart.

Robert is a consultant in Cardiology and Lifestyle Medicine. He came to HPC to shift from being a doctor to a coach, and he needed help with launching his business online. He wanted to offer health and lifestyle coaching to existing patients to add value to his practice.

'In healthcare, it becomes apparent that most patients don't listen or are overloaded by all the information I give them,' Robert said.

'The only option is to show them how to improve their own health. This led me to provide coaching programs.'

Robert wasn't sure how to transition the conversation from doctor and patient to talking about his coaching programs. He was in a unique position of having potential patients already attending his clinic whom he could invite to a free session and yet was finding himself a little stuck.

How Do I Create a High-Paying Client?

We've now gone through some of what it takes internally for you to build your business, which is your Unshakeable Belief in your business, clients, and yourself. We'll continue to develop this throughout the book. And it's important to note that this job is never done; there's always another deeper layer — a mountain with no top that we learn to love to climb.

We've looked at how to lay and build upon those foundations with your niche, messaging, method, and high-fee program. You're well on your way to being a High-Performing Coach!

Now it's time for the next piece in creating extraordinary results and high-paying clients — **your performance and how to empower your clients to help clients say YES!**

Why Performance?

Lots of people think performance is the outcome.

It's not.

Performance is the actions you take or don't take.

Let's look at what it would take for a tennis player to win Wimbledon.

She needs to have a great level of performance: mastery in her serve, volley, backhand, forehand, cross-court, tactics, and strategy. The more she practises, the better a player she will be. Then, assuming her internal game (thinking) is as developed as her outer game (actions) and many other physical factors, maybe one day she'll win Wimbledon.

For coaches, we've got to know the performance for us to win the games we are playing, creating high-fee clients, leaving a lasting difference in our clients' lives, and building a thriving business.

- What are the actions to take?

- What is the strategy?

A coach's performance ultimately boils down to one single word: CONVERSATIONS.

It's a conversation that leads your clients through a powerful experience with intentionality ...

And has a purpose to serve and make a difference in people's lives as they embark on their own personal and professional journey.

No conversations? No business.

And it's not just any old conversation. It's an extraordinarily powerful conversation I call the Breakthrough Process.

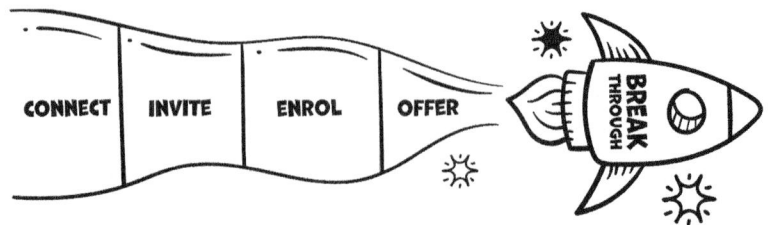

Essential Element 3: The Breakthrough Process

When I worked with Rich Litvin, I had no real idea how to create high-fee clients. It was a mystery to me, and I felt frustrated because I'd been coaching for years but had never built a coaching business.

Working with Rich transformed my business and my life. **He taught me a process called 'connect, invite, create, propose equals clients'.** That made total sense to me. I loved it because I'm process-driven. I take the steps and practise getting good at them, and big outcomes follow.

The more coaching calls I made, the more I started to see patterns. It wasn't enough just to coach clients on their challenges; they needed inspiration, a new vision for life that would light them up. This is what creates enrolment — when you leave a person inspired and believing they can have the life they've always dreamed of.

But no matter how well I enrolled clients in this brighter vision, it often wasn't enough. Once money entered the conversation, a lot of resistance and fear would show up. I realised it wasn't enough just to propose. It had to be more than that; otherwise, I'd be stuck playing the 'Yes/No' game.

I stood for transformation and breakthroughs — the only game I ever want to play. I wanted to show up in such a way that I could powerfully create the results I wanted to create and help my clients create the results they wanted to create too — total alignment. Achieving this is surprisingly simple …

So, when clients resisted the very thing they said they wanted, I would help them have a BREAKTHROUGH instead.

After hundreds of calls, I naturally found and evolved my own process beyond what I'd learned from Rich, developing new ideas around some of the early parts of his process and then amending other aspects entirely, with a significant increase in results for my business and my clients.

Below are my five steps for a coach who wants to create extraordinary results for themself and their clients, becoming a High-Performing Coach.

The Breakthrough Process: Connect, Invite, Enrol, Offer, Breakthrough.

In this chapter, we will focus on connecting and inviting. In Chapter 7, we will cover Enrol, Offer, and Breakthrough.

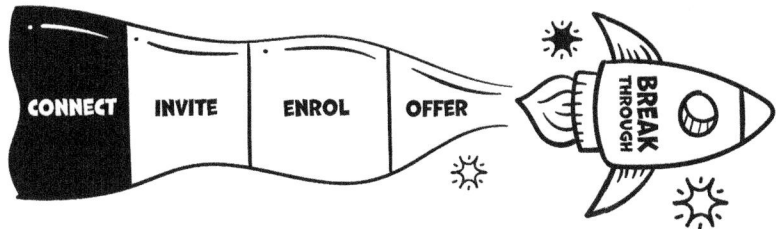

Breakthrough Process, Step 1: Connect

We've got to know how to connect with people in an authentic, real, and sincere way. Then we must understand how to lead conversations powerfully in service of our clients. We've got to know where to go to have those conversations, whom to have them with, and how to have them be intentional, meaningful and make a difference.

Connection has to feel real. You can't force it or fake it. There are many secrets to building our kind of business, but one of them is genuinely connecting in an authentic, open way, at a heart-to-heart level, in total alignment with who we are and what we stand for. Show up from this space, and this connection is felt deeply and effortlessly. When done with enough skill, it leads us into invitation — inviting clients to a coaching conversation where we can go deeper and serve.

When we've established some compelling reason to spend more time with a potential client, we can see and feel that there's a way we can help them, and we communicate this clearly. They'll feel that buzz too. Your invitations will most often be met with a 'Yes, that sounds amazing!'

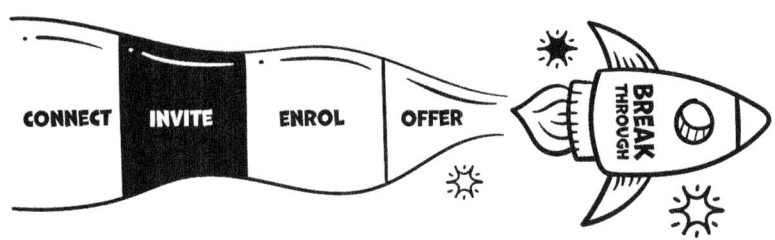

Breakthrough Process, Step 2: Invite

We extend our invitation WITHOUT attachment, giving people a space they can choose to move into or not.

Invite them to have a session with you. You might call it a discovery call, a clarity call, or a breakthrough call — whatever you like — it's essentially a coaching conversation. Your aim is to invite someone to a conversation where you can powerfully support and empower them to confront their challenges, so they're able to see a path to having the positive outcome their heart truly desires. You cannot sell coaching, but you can give someone a powerful experience. This takes away the need for selling, convincing, and all those tactics that just don't work in this world or feel aligned within ourselves anyway.

Where Do I Find Clients to Connect With?

Out of all the questions and confusion new coaches have, this is probably the biggest.

Want to know the BEST way to find clients and launch and grow your business?

Talk to the people right in front of you!

It's the people you already know, the new people you meet — they're in your Facebook and WhatsApp groups, you studied with them or met them on another program, you work with them or did in the past, they are your friends — the people you see and interact with online and offline. There's something about them; you're drawn to them, or there's nothing about them because you really don't know them much at all — it's the curiosity that creates the opening ...

And because of the way you are showing up — open, honest, vulnerable, curious, genuine, unattached, and altogether great — they feel drawn to you too. **This is your personal network, and this is the most powerful place to start.**

Your network

When it comes to strategy, there are two camps for creating clients. The first is everybody you already know — your first-degree connections, a.k.a. your personal network, as we've just described. They are one message, voice note, email, phone call, or conversation away from creating an opening for something extraordinary to happen.

The second camp is the rest of the world. If you want to connect with them, you've got to create content and build Online Influence so they can find you. If you have a strategy for both, then you've got a great opportunity to rapidly build your business. We'll look at how you can grow your audience, tapping into the second camp through your content strategy, which we'll discuss later in this book.

Your personal network is so effective because established relationships are already there. It's called the know, like, trust factor, and it's a perfect starting point for connecting with potential clients.

In my first two years, I built a profitable business just from my personal network.

At one stage, I was starting around 60 connecting conversations a week, booking 5–10 enrolment calls and creating 1–3 new clients most weeks. My business was moving, my client list was growing, and I was gaining invaluable experience.

It's worth mentioning that at this stage, I had no online presence and was coaching part-time for the first 12 months as I was winding down my fitness business. This will help you to understand the power of the Breakthrough Process alone and apply it to your personal network.

Leveraging your personal network is the most effective way to launch your coaching business and start creating high-paying clients with velocity. I know plenty of successful coaches who never change their approach and have $100K+ businesses, many of whom are our clients.

In a recent poll, we asked our 800+ clients where their first high-paying client came from, having come through our training. A whopping 58 percent came from this strategy, 26 percent from online content, and 11 percent from connecting with people they didn't know.

Getting Connected

Before having that coaching session and beginning an enrolment process, we need to learn how to connect with people we would love to serve.

Clients often ask for tips on how to approach potential clients. Initially, I simply ask them to write down the names of people they know, for whom they would love to explore the possibility of making a difference. I ask them to tell me the person's first name and then I ask, 'Why them?' This is to help them get connected, in their own hearts and minds, to why they wanted to talk to this person.

Then I'll always ask, 'If you were going to be authentic and great, and speak from your heart, what would you say?' This always stops them in their tracks. What normally comes out of their mouth is something so real and rich that the listener is left feeling inspired. The secret to starting conversations is to be authentic and really great with people in your approach.

Imagine yourself like a bright beaming light, deeply grounded in who you are — what you're about and the value you bring. There is an innate quality in this — it's high-vibrational. This is what High-Performing Coaches do and how they show up.

I'll give you an example from my business (which also demonstrates the enormous value already hiding in your close network).

When I was building my business, there was someone in my life called Dave. We had worked together in a previous life and always stayed in touch. He ran a successful London agency, and I knew Dave valued leadership, was ambitious, and was taking personal development programs with a desire to bringing this to his team and company culture. So, I sent him a message:

Hi Dave! I was thinking about you! How are you!? I haven't spoken to you in ages. I wanted to let you know I'm building my coaching business now. I know how much you value leadership and growth, and having your people get trained and developed, so I wanted to reach out to you. Up for a chat?

Five minutes later, he texted back:

Sounds great, Ryan. Are you free in half an hour?

After the initial 'Hello/how are you doing/great to speak to you', I changed gears in the conversation. I asked what was happening in his company, what his biggest challenge was, how it had been impacting the business, how long it had been that way, and what he'd love instead. I listened and held space as he answered, and in just ten minutes, he was left with more insight into his situation. I could hear his enthusiasm grow as he shared just a sense of what he really wanted. I also listened for clarity on where I thought I could help.

Then I asked him if he was open to having help making it happen, and he said yes without hesitation.

The next day we met for breakfast, something I'd never done before or since, but due to our connection, this felt good for me. During breakfast, I said, 'Look, tell me more about those challenges.'

We went deep into his specific challenges and how they were affecting him and his business. I gave him some on-the-spot coaching around how he could be more authentic in his communication. We explored the route of avoiding communicating important issues, where it came from, and how it leaves him feeling.

'What's opening up for you?' I asked from time to time, giving him a chance to reflect and get connected to whatever he was present to.

We explored his vision more: what his business could be if he showed up more in open, honest, authentic communication. I saw his power return before my eyes, and he told me, 'I think it would be great for you to have a session with one of my business partners.'

I said, 'Yes, of course, I'd love to, and can I also ask, are you open to doing the work too and getting committed to investing your time and energy to make that vision happen, from the top down? If you approached it like this, how do you think that would go?'

A week later, I started working with one of his directors, and soon after that I began work with him and one of his other directors. A month after that, another director. A month after that, I was coaching his whole team. I worked with Dave's company for two years before I changed direction in my business, generating £2K–£4K a month from this relationship.

As their ambitions grew, they were ready to play an even bigger game. I could see they needed more precise expertise, so I suggested they find an expert specific to their industry. Through mutual agreement, I stepped away soon after as they took their business to the next level. It was an impactful, long, rewarding engagement for us all.

All this growth and impact from sending one text message and getting connected.

One of our clients once posted on social media: 'Hey, I'm practising my enrolment calls for building my coaching business as a really powerful, deep coaching session. Who would like to have a free session?'

She created 20+ enrolment conversations, and a consistent flow of clients, one of whom became a huge corporate client, and she generated over €70,000 in four months.

Another client, Steph, began connection messages that were less direct, sharing what he was up to, who he helps, and asking, 'Know anyone like that?' He created over £50K in three months.

I love it when our clients share their success with our community. Everyone learns and everyone wins — as I said, this is a collaboration.

Find the Right Approach

When you start your connecting conversation, imagine it like a range. There's a range in terms of how direct you might want to be, depending on the relationship and your audience. I advise you to look at it case by case. One approach might be absolutely appropriate for a relationship you have, and that same approach might be completely inappropriate for another.

It's vital that you approach each individual in a way that feels good for you. If it feels good for you because you gave it a little thought, chances are high that it will work for other people too. Personally, I've always had more success in my personal network by being more on the direct side. I've found that when creating new connections, a gentler approach works better. Every audience is unique.

Think about some people in your network right now. Take a moment to write down three names and ask yourself, 'Who would I love to connect with, and who would I love to explore the possibility of making a difference to? Why are they on my list? Is that the kind of relationship I can be more direct with, or less direct?' Trust your instincts, be authentic, be great, get in your heart, and have a go.

Harriet is another example of a connection from my personal network. She is an artist. We met at a Course in Miracles workshop back in 2009 and kept in touch over the years. She came straight to mind when I asked myself, 'Who would I love to connect with and explore the possibility of making a difference to?'

I sent Harriet a message:

Hey Harriet, how are you!? It's been a while and I was thinking about you. I have just started building my coaching business and I'm helping people break through whatever is stopping them — it's really exciting! What are you up to these days?

She came back with:

Hey Ryan, it's great to hear from you! I'm busy in my art studio getting ready for my next exhibition. It's going great. Your coaching business sounds exciting. I'd love to hear more!

I invited her to a call, and we had a brief connecting conversation, simply catching up. Then I changed gears in the conversation, because I wanted to make it more meaningful for both of us.

'So, I shared with you in my text about my coaching business and how I am helping people with whatever is stopping them. I wanted to find out a bit more about what you are up to and where you are at — see how I could help you. Does that sound good?'

She said yes, and I asked her more about her art, what she was creating in her life, her challenges, how they were impacting her, and what she'd love to have instead. She shared that her biggest challenge was around men. She felt she had some blocks around her parents and certain childhood events. Her career was going well, but what she wanted was to feel ready for love and meet the man of her dreams. As I listened, I knew I could help her in some meaningful way.

I played back what I heard her say, and then I asked: 'Are you open to having help with that?'

She said she was, and I invited her to have a session with me, which sounded like: 'I'd love to invite you to have a deeper session with me for us to explore this more. We'll flush out what's getting in your way, get even clearer about what you want to create, and explore some strategies on how to bring it more to life. Then we can go from there. Either way, I promise you that this will be a powerful experience for you. How does that sound?'

This was a session that I offered her without charge. I didn't even mention that it was free, and I never do. I keep money completely out of my invitations and focus on the real intention: to serve.

After she told me, 'This sounds amazing', we agreed to meet the next day, where we went deep and I took her through my Unshakeable Belief Process, coached her around her challenges and blocks and how we could work together, what that would look like, and what the investment would be.

By the end of that day, she had transferred £4,000 to start her journey. After our first six months together, Harriet and I continued our coaching relationship for another six months at the same rate.

In that time, we unpacked and completed much of her past around her mum and dad and stripped away her fears around her own self-worth. With my support, she faced some of her deepest shadows and learned how to integrate them more. At one point, she even had the bravery to jump out of a plane! By the end of our time together, Harriet was still looking for love but was more ready than ever.

A block for many coaches is the pressure they put themselves under to produce results for their clients. Often, that fear paralyses them so much that they even withhold an offer to work together.

However, it's important to understand our clients' results are not our responsibility. Coaches don't produce any results for our clients; results and outcomes are based on the actions clients take. This is their responsibility.

As coaches, we create a space for new insights, new beliefs, and new actions.

- We hold our clients accountable for their greatness.

- We are gentle and firm.

- We have their backs.

- We lead.

- We guide.

- We allow.

We trust the process and understand our clients will get exactly what they're ready to get. This in itself will be highly valuable to them. With this understanding, we are free to serve without pressure or attachment to those things outside our control.

Coaching is not a done-for-you service. It's not a guaranteed result or money-back type offering. What would our clients learn if it were? To continue to rely on someone else to 'fix' their deepest challenges. Only they can break through their own challenges. Our job is to believe and to trust, both in ourselves and in our clients.

Coaching is about empowering our clients to get to their own vast potential. To help them unlock all the power inside of them, so they can discover who they truly are, step into their greatness, and take effective action.

Yes, the quality of the coaching will have a profound effect on client outcomes. Don't let that mess with your head. Trust that you can deliver an extraordinarily valuable experience and can make a difference over and over and over again with different clients. In this process, you will grow, cultivate Unshakeable Belief, and become a greater coach with even greater impact.

What if I told you that one of the most powerful break-throughs I ever helped a client have was the time I said absolutely nothing at all. For 20 minutes, all I did was listen, hold space, be fully present and patient. He felt safe, and I knew he just needed some room to go within and get what was there for him to get. It was a coaching session like no other! I'm a master at holding space, and you want to become a master at this too.

Connect — Changing the Gear

Small talk is the enemy of an intentional, meaningful, connecting conversation.

When connecting, getting too caught up in the weather/world politics/what you just watched on Netflix dilutes the impact of your call and your impact as a coach. Fail to lead the conversation and make it meaningful, and your potential client will take over and lead it far away, in a direction far from the one you intended. This can be super frustrating, and usually what comes from these types of conversations is little more than 'It was nice to connect with you!'

Quite far removed from the transformation you wanted to create at the start, isn't it?

Once you've said hi and created that initial connection, we want to change the gear in that conversation. Make it intentional and lead it.

Feeling into when is the appropriate time to change the gear comes with practice, experience, and presence.

Changing the gear changes the way the person is listening and steers the conversation in a direction that could be significant in that individual's life. We are opening up a space for you to take it where you want it to go — where it's impactful and transformative.

Changing the gear can look as simple as:

Hey, it's so great to catch up with you and reconnect! Since we last spoke, I've been building my coaching business, and it's been so rewarding. I'm working with high-achieving men and women who want to live with a deeper sense of purpose. I know you have been doing so great in your life and career already, and I'm also curious to hear more about what's next for you? What's the deeper sense of purpose you are creating or would love to create?

I changed the gear with Harriet. "So, I shared with you in my text about my coaching business and how I am helping people with whatever is stopping them. I wanted to find out a bit more about what you are up to and where you are at — see how I could help you. Does that sound good?"

In my first message to Dave, the gear was already high.

Showing up in a conversation like that creates authority and confidence in you as the wise and trusted guide. If they're not open to that, they'll say so, and you can take the conversation in another direction.

If you want to take one step before changing gear, try:

Hey, listen, there's something I wanted to share with you. I wanted to check if you're open to hearing about it?

This will create some intrigue and give them a chance to open. Then they can say, 'Oh yeah, I'd love to hear', to which your reply will be: 'OK. Well, look, I've been building my business. I'm helping people create more purpose in their life. I was really curious, what are you up to? What's your big mission in the world?' They'll start sharing what they're excited about. **People love talking about what is in their hearts.**

You can also add in a technique where you ask for permission, which looks like:

Hey, it's so great to catch up with you. Since we last spoke, I've been building my coaching business — working with men who would like to fulfil their purpose. I wanted to find out more about you and what you're up to. Does that feel good to share with me? If so, I'd love to hear what you're working on. What's your big dream for the year?

Here's that same example again, with a subtle difference:

Hey, it's so great to catch up with you. Since we last spoke, I've been building my coaching business. I'm working with men and women who are dreaming about fulfilling a greater sense of purpose in their lives, and I thought about you! I'd love to know your big mission in the world if you're up for sharing it with me?

Do you see how natural, unattached, non-threatening, and enticing we make the conversation when we change the gear like this? Not to mention that we're now taking it somewhere useful and potentially life-changing!

Validation

When someone opens up and shares passionately about their life, what's in their minds, hearts, and what they really care about, it's important not only to listen but to also let them know you get it — this is called validation, and there are few things better in the world than being heard, gotten, seen, and understood in this way. It's such a sweet gift for the person who just opened up. This also deepens the connection.

'Wow, you must be so excited, and I can feel your passion, it's infectious! I really get your commitment to living your best life and using all your experience to create something great for yourself, your life, and all those who will benefit from what you will create! Thank you for sharing that with me.'

'When I heard you share, I was really touched by your determination and the willingness to take a stand for what you want and really go for it. I love what you are up to!'

'I'm hearing how much this means to you and how much you care, and I really get how much time, energy, and effort you have already put into this — you have a lot to offer, and I'm genuinely excited for you!'

On the flip side, it's always disappointing when we share our hearts out and the person responds with the next question — like they didn't get it at all! This creates disconnect.

It goes without saying that your response should be genuine and authentic. Don't make up compliments or fake charm them; be real and speak from your heart like they just did.

A sense of vision

The next step might be something like, 'How would you absolutely love all this to go?' That's a great question because now we're getting them into a powerfully inspiring imaginative and visionary state. We're getting them out of what they may have been stuck in or only dreaming about, and we're helping them get connected to what they truly desire and what that would feel like. That conversation starts to create more excitement, more enthusiasm, more enrolment.

'Well, I'd love to see myself being on a beach, working from my laptop, making a difference to people, having more time for myself, and having a more peaceful lifestyle.'

'I want to build something that gives me total freedom to enjoy my work on my own terms and have time for my family. I want my future to have more balance, play, fun, and fulfilment too!'

Create an opening

Once they share a sense of their vision, you might want to offer more validation again and create an opening for what's next: 'I love the sound of that, and I can feel how much having that would mean to you. I'm curious to know, are you open to having help to make all that happen?'

This is the million-dollar-impact question. We can only help people who are open to receiving help. If they're not open, that's OK. You can maybe say, 'OK. If you're not open, I hear you; can you tell me a bit more?' Then they might tell you something that can open up the conversation a little bit.

Invite

When you hear yes, and you know your potential client is open to having some help, you want to invite them to have a session with you in such a way that your potential client is left feeling that this invitation is a real opportunity for them and, at the same time, with a great sense of openness around accepting your invitation or not — that it's really OK for them to say no.

If they are open, say: *Great, I want to invite you to have a session with me because, based on everything you shared with me, I think I can make a difference to help you see how you can bring all this to life. We'll go deeper into your vision, we'll flush out the things that might stand in your way, we'll explore the best kind of strategy that you can act on right away ... Then we can go from there. I promise, if nothing else, it's going to be a really powerful experience for you. How does that sound?*

Now, when you're connected and you have helped somebody get present with their dreams, what they truly want to create, and they are offered real help to make it happen, most people say yes. At that point, you can schedule your first call together, then and there.

If that person shows any sign of resistance and starts to worry about cost, there's a simple way to put their mind at ease:

There's no cost to this. This is a gift from me to you. I want to give you a powerful experience, so here's my invitation. My process is to take you through a coaching session designed to give you real value where we get to focus entirely on you, with nothing else getting in the way. Then we can see what starts to open up for you, and then we can literally just take it from there. Open to trusting the process?

In doing this, you create relief and a sense of safety for your client to move forward without pressure on them, or some sense of expectation from you, or feelings of guilt on their part. If there's still resistance, explore that. If it's not for them, it's not for them. You're not there to convince anybody. You're exploring with that person to see what flows. If something is flowing in this direction, you can facilitate it. If it's flowing in another direction, you can facilitate that. Either way, you're unattached and standing for something to be possible for them. That's how you connect and invite.

'You're not open? Hey, I completely get that and it's totally OK to say no. In fact, one of the things I help people with is being authentic and free to express themselves authentically, so I want to thank you for being that way with me. AND look, if anything ever changes, I'd love to hear from you.'

Make it really OK and thank them for whatever they say.

Creating Unshakeable Belief Around Connecting and Inviting

In previous chapters, we discussed Unshakeable Belief. Beliefs you have about yourself, potential clients, and your business. If they're false, limiting, unconscious beliefs, they'll hold you back.

When it comes to connecting and inviting, here are some beliefs of yours that might be showing up.

They'll think I'm trying to sell them something: Think along these lines, and you're going to create a lot of resistance for yourself to the idea of starting a conversation. Remember the distinction: **Serving vs. Selling.**

They won't want to pay for my coaching: This is putting them in a box — deciding what your clients can and cannot do. That is the opposite of what coaching is about. Avoid projecting what's in your mind onto your clients. Remember the distinction: **It can be done, and you can do it! So can your clients!**

They might say no. I don't want to be rejected: This is when your brain gets very clever. If you believe you're not good enough, and that ultimately you're going to experience failure, then all your brain is going to want to do is keep you safe from experiencing that pain. Remember the distinction: **It's about them, not you.**

If you believe people will say no, or that they cannot do something, and you make that personal, your brain will also decide there's no point and stop you from taking actions that would otherwise get you closer to your goals. Your brain won't put you in a place it thinks is guaranteed to hurt you. That's just your brain doing its job.

Ultimately, what's going on in the background is that your identity is at risk and your mind is trying its best to protect you from itself. It keeps you safe with all of these beliefs, but it's a trap. As soon as we get lost to our worries or project our worries onto others, we're no longer coaching.

The art of being a High-Performing Coach is, you don't project stories, views, or opinions onto your clients. Instead, you make a space for your own internal noise, observe, let it go, and create space for better thoughts. **You free yourself, and you see your clients more as the infinite possibility that they are. You have Unshakeable Belief in yourself and in your clients.**

Right here, right now is a great time to start exploring what's standing between you and Unshakeable Belief. All your false beliefs — showing up right here in the connect and invite stage — the made-up stories you're telling yourself. They keep you stuck, small, and a long way from positively impacting people, let alone creating clients. The first step is to acknowledge it, then understand the reality that none of those thoughts are true. If you can do this, you're well on your way to creating Unshakeable Belief, connecting, inviting, and creating your first, or your next, high-paying client!

High-fee clients are everywhere

It might not feel like it right now, but once you're familiar with my process, your eyes will be trained to see that there really are high-fee clients everywhere in your day-to-day life.

Let me give you an example.

I was standing next to a guy at the back of an event, and the speaker was talking about posting and creating content, when the guy remarked, 'You know, I never post online.'

I asked him why, and he replied, 'You know …' I could sense he was open, and he started to share: 'I just feel like I don't want anybody to think I'm desperate for business, like I'm needy and all those things. So, I just don't post online.'

He had already started sharing his challenge, which was that he didn't want people to think he was desperate. Switching into coach mode, I gave him some validation and started leading the conversation. I asked: 'Ahh, so you don't want to appear needy because you don't want people to get the wrong idea about you? How's all that impacting you and your business? What's the impact of this challenge and what you just shared with me?'

'Well, yeah, it's definitely impacted me because there's a lot of people I'm connected to online, and I know they would love to have me help them, but they never get to find out about me because I just don't show up. I can see it's kind of bothering me in the background because I want to be better than that. It's impacted me financially, it's impacting me mentally, and it's impacting me emotionally.'

'Wow, that's a lot. I see there are obviously a lot of impacts there for you. How long has it been that way?'

He had to think, and then …

'Wow. Since I started my business.'

'OK, how long has that been?'

'Six years ago.'

'Wow. I get it! It sounds like you've been dealing with this for a long time, and I get the sense you'd like to break through it somehow. Can I ask you what would you love to have instead?'

At this point, bear in mind, we didn't even know each other's names. This is just what it looks like when you're open, allowing, and able to lead conversations with skill.

'I'd love to be able to just be free and just post stuff online that would help people learn more about how I can help them and learn more about how they can get the kind of things that they need regarding this particular area of building a business. Yeah, I would just love to do that. I'd love to be out there more.'

'Great. I can feel the concern as you say all that but also the desire and the willingness. Are you open to having any help with that?'

'Yes, I think so. But why are you asking?'

'I'm a coach, and I help entrepreneurs get clear of all the things that are getting in their way so they can go build whatever it is that they want to build. Having listened to you, what you're dealing with, and what you would love to have, I know I could help you. That's why I wanted to know if you're open to having any help.'

'Wow, I can't believe we've ended up having this conversation. I'm open. What's involved?'

'If you're open, that's great. I'd love to invite you to have a Zoom session with me, and we'll spend about an hour together. We'll go deeper into what's going on in the background. I'll help you get clear about it. We'll get even clearer about your vision and what you would love to have for your business. Then we can go from there. Whatever happens, I promise you, it's going to be of great value. It's going to make a big difference for you.'

'Sounds great. Let's book it in.' We pulled out our phones at the same time and scheduled it there and then.

Two days later, at 2 pm on a Thursday, we had our call where I helped him get clarity, have insights, and achieve breakthroughs.

I offered to work together for eight weeks.

Five minutes later, he'd transferred £4,000 into my account.

This is how powerfully and rapidly the Connect, Invite, Enrol, Offer, Breakthrough process can work.

Connect/Invite: A Deeper Understanding

During the initial connect/invite conversation, I have found it extremely effective to inquire lightly into the challenges potential clients are facing and the impact of those challenges.

This serves two purposes:

1. It helps our potential clients get more present to those challenges and where it's leaving them. This is powerful in and of itself.

2. It helps us to be clearer if and how we can help our clients. If they are challenged by something we feel we're not the best placed to help with, this can help us direct the conversation in a way that's more appropriate for them. If we hear we can help solve the particular challenge, we are given more energy to keep leading the conversation in a confident and deliberate way.

If, for any reason, using that word, 'challenge', doesn't resonate with you, get creative and use words or phrases that feel better for you. The more you understand this process-within-a-process, the more your creativity will flow.

1. Your clients have something that they want and do not have — find out what that is:

- What's the one thing you want more than anything that you do not currently have?

- What's the change you want to see in your life?

- What are you up to creating in your life by the end of this year?

- What's the big vision?

- What's your game for the year?

2. There's a reason they don't have it already — they're stuck on something, something is missing, or something is in the way. Helping them see that and get present to it will create awareness in your client. You need to understand it too, so you can be clear on whether you can help or not.

- What's your greatest challenge in bringing it to life?

- What's the main thing stopping you from having it?

- What's getting in your way?

- What's missing?

3. They need to experience a sense of truth around their pains/frustrations — because this is real. When you want something and don't have it AND you are blocked in some way — there's an impact. Let's get present to that.

- How's that been impacting you?

- What's it been like for you?

- How is this affecting you and the other parts of your life?

4. I love asking 'How long has it been that way?' to help us both get even more present to the reality. Sometimes people have been stuck with this for years, and they never share that with anyone. If it's new, it always gives you perspective on how to serve them.

5. Then it's time to imagine a future and get present to that, leaving them feeling more enrolled and inspired.

   - What would you love to have happen instead?
   - If you could wave a magic wand, what would it look like?
   - If you had the most incredible year, what result would you love to create?

6. Go ahead and proceed with the Invite set-up.

   - Are you open to having any help?

As they say yes, they're actually saying yes to themselves having what they want, and this is already hugely valuable.

7. The Invite:

   - Well, I'd love to invite you to have a session with me. We'll go deeper into what's getting in your way, look at your strategy, stretch your vision, and leave you clearer on what it's going to take and how you can make it happen. This will be a powerful experience for you one way or another. And then we can go from there. Sound good?

You don't need to follow these words like a script. I'm delivering them here to help you understand the mechanics.

Use them or create your own. Find what works for you best and see what happens.

A final word on the Connect/Invite conversation: this is not a deep dive. Keep it light. Our intention here is just to get a sense of things. It might look like a long process, but this entire conversation can be done in a few minutes only, and for this light exploration, the shorter the better. What's important is that in just a few minutes, your potential client becomes present to what's alive in them and what they want that they do not have. In doing that, you have left them more enrolled in themselves, their own vision, and in you. All of a sudden, they can't wait to have that call with you!

I have led this very conversation, in person and via text, email, Zoom, mobile, WhatsApp, Messenger, and at events thousands of times — the results have been astounding!

Your approach will adapt and evolve. For now, these are your training wheels. Keep the bits you like, leave the parts you don't like, practise, practise, and allow it to evolve in your own way. If you take this on, it will transform your business, your life, and the lives of your clients.

A Word to the Wise on Paid Advertising

So, I have to actually talk to people? And what about funnels, landing pages, and paid advertising?

There are essentially two sources where you can connect with potential clients, or — as they are referred to in the marketing world — sources of traffic.

1. Organic

2. Paid

Your personal network is accessible organically right now and is only a message, phone call, text, or conversation away. The conversation can move fast, with potentially fast results.

Creating your Online Influence, sharing content that deeply connects and offers real value to your audience and also widens your network by opening you up to second-degree connections and beyond is also highly effective — we'll go more into this in Chapter 8.

Paid advertising is by far one of the most effective ways to reach more people and grow and scale a business. However, it's also the most expensive and one of the most challenging to make work. Timing is everything here, and the operative word is 'scale'.

Often coaches take this path before they are ready, trying to scale a business that simply is not ready to be scaled. It's a bit like walking into a Formula 1 car before you have passed your driving test. You're simply not ready. You have yet to gather the experience required to 'safely' drive it.

The most effective way to launch, grow, test, verify, and validate a new or 'launching' coaching business is leveraging your personal network.

If you are looking to get clarity on whether to use paid advertising yet or not, let me make it simple for you:

1. Are you well on your way to cultivating Unshakeable Belief in yourself, your coaching, and your business?

    Yes   No

2. Are your Business Foundations solid, tested, and verified, including niche, messaging, and high-fee program?

    Yes   No

3. Do you have a track record of effectiveness in your enrolment calls (25+ percent conversion)?

   Yes   No

4. Do you have a strong online presence in place for the new potential clients entering into your world through paid advertising who'll want to find out more about you?

   Yes   No

5. Are you ready and able to invest around a minimum of $1K–$5K each and every month in marketers and advertising spend (bearing in mind it could take anything from 3 to 6 months to get this working, if at all)?

   Yes   No

If you answered yes to all of those questions, then I say you are ready to scale using paid advertising if you feel drawn to it.

For most, if not all, new coaches or coaches who are under-performing in their business, their answers will be mostly no, and that's why the *word to the wise* is to avoid paid advertising strategies until you are ready and can say yes to each of the above questions. How do you get to that point? Follow every-thing laid out in this book.

Summary of other organic connection strategies

To give you more juice for your creative brain, here is a list of other ways to connect — including, but not limited to, your direct and personal first-degree connections.

See which ones light you up the most and start from there.

- Personal network

- WhatsApp groups
- Social media network
- Other social media groups (think about the places your audience congregates)
- Your own community you've created
- Online networking groups, workshops, and meetups
- Offline networking groups, workshops, and meetups
- Client referrals (be bold and ask your clients if they know anyone they'd love to share your work with)
- Sharing wisdom and inspiration through online content
- Run a free/low-fee 2-hour workshop
- Run a full-day experience, event, or workshop
- Run a challenge
- Comment on and engage with other people's content
- Share wisdom and unique points of view, and add value in every interaction
- Local/free press
- Website
- Your own podcast
- Make your presence more visible on Google
- Current client renewals/extensions
- Guest on other people's stages (groups, podcasts, workshops, events, or summits)
- Share high-value free content: blueprints/swipe files/ top strategies

- Write your book (recommended when you have validated and established your business first, not before)

- Create more fun ways of connecting with people such as themed social meetups, for example, wine-tasting events (what would be fun for you would be fun for others, and people are drawn to fun)

Go to www.ryanmathie.com/book and access a live training I held online on Connect, Invite and changing the gear.

Robert's Breakthrough

We showed Robert how simple it could be to invite his patients to a different conversation by changing the gear, connecting, and inviting, and he applied it right away. This worked so well that after a matter of a few weeks, he had already enrolled twelve people in his first-ever group coaching program. During an eight-week program, Robert had successfully transformed their health as well as many sources of their stress.

'This first program covered my HPC joining fee and costs,' he says.

'I quickly realised that getting connections right, and showing up as me, was the only way to invite clients to a free conversation and then convert them to paid participants in my program. Initially, I just got stuck in, messy, and tried.'

'I had to be me and deal with any of my internal issues, so those limiting beliefs did not affect the calls. I struggled until I broke through to the next level of complete self-acceptance and self-compassion. After that, dealing with any potential client call was so much easier. I listened to everyone and resisted jumping in (like a doctor), and very soon I had my second group program, which is almost full already.'

For Robert, working through the Five Essential Elements and implementing them in his business brought his professional career as a doctor 'up a notch'.

'I had many patients right in front of me every day. I just wasn't sure how to transition the conversation from where it was to a potential coaching conversation, so understanding how to change the gears and invite made a real difference fast!

'Coaching and listening to patients really transforms their health and well-being, even more than all the medications and procedures do. It also comes with huge personal satisfaction as a doctor and coach to be able to make such a huge difference in people's lives.

'Without HPC and the Five Essentials, I would likely still be chasing my tail trying to work out how to start, spending even more money and likely giving up on my dreams.

'Now I have the confidence to launch as a coach, to achieve breakthrough calls, to succeed and grow.'

Unshakeable Belief in his inner self and his abilities, and sharing that with those he wanted to serve, brought a whole new level of abundance to everything he does.

Robert is a Cardiologist AND a Health Coach. His business is now thriving and sustainable. He couldn't be more satisfied with the added value and difference he gets to make to his patients.

Exercise:
Feel Your Unshakeable Belief

What's a new powerfully aligned Unshakeable Belief you can create for yourself right now about connecting with people?

> For example: 'People want to hear from me, and I have a huge difference to make!'

How does that feel?

> How about: 'There are so many people dealing with the kinds of challenges I am good at helping people solve, and I'm open to connecting with people and trusting that it will all come together!'

How does that one feel?

What's a new, powerfully aligned Unshakeable Belief you can create for yourself right now about inviting people to a call?

> For example: 'I can make a difference to this person, and I want to create a simple pathway to be able to do that.'

How does that one feel?

> How about: 'It's OK if they say no. At least I am giving myself and people the chance, and I trust that if I invite people and open myself up, things will start to flow!'

How does that one feel?

What's a new, powerfully aligned Unshakeable Belief you can create for yourself right now about actually having your enrolment call?

For example, 'This call could be the most important call of this person's life. I'm going to show up fully, hold nothing back, and be great and straight!'

How does that one feel?

How about: 'I'm so grateful for the honour of being able to dig deep into someone's life. I will show up with respect and gratitude and all my power to serve this person to the best of my ability.'

How does that one feel?

These are the very same beliefs I created for myself. They worked for me and so many of our clients. See what works for you, use them, and create your own so you are left feeling free and motivated to take action!

7
Breakthrough Process, Part II:
Enrol, Offer, Breakthrough

A process of creation and a new vision declared.
A choice to believe, that must be chosen and
believed, moment by moment, over and over again.

Kelly is a Dating and Relationship Coach who helps divorced singles find The One and build an extraordinary relationship through online program.

'I was running another business when I joined HPC and was coaching on the side. I had a number of private clients, but I wasn't able to consistently attract new clients or build a business from coaching.'

Kelly had an incredible track record of successfully helping her clients work through the blocks they had to creating healthy, lasting relationships. She believed in her ability to create life-changing experiences for her clients, and she was excited about the potential of her work. She was determined and hungry to find a way to help more people find happiness, peace, and a love that could last.

Despite her success, Kelly had doubts about what she could create in her coaching business. She also had a tendency to people-please. She was unclear about the best way to position her business, her fees, where to find clients, and how to respond to money blocks ...

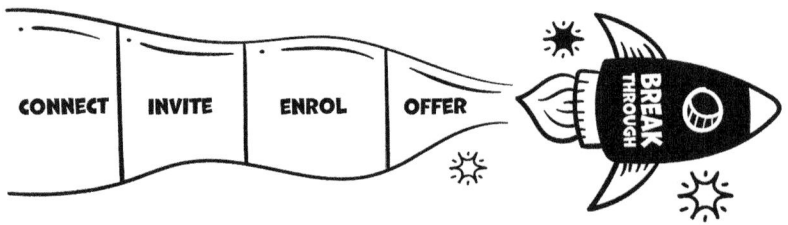

Breakthrough Process: Connect, Invite, Enrol, Offer, Breakthrough

To recap, after we have connected authentically and meaningfully, we can take it to the next part, which is to invite people to have a coaching session. The best approach is to offer people a free opportunity to experience working with you. Once they spend time with you, they can discover for themselves what coaching is and the difference it can make, and then you go from there.

Let's move on to Step 3 in the Breakthrough Process ...

It's time to bring all your magic and do what you love the most: coach!

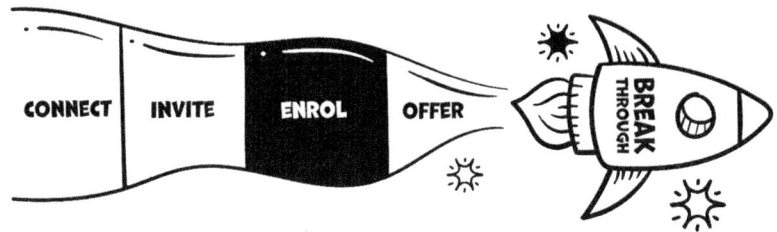

Breakthrough Process, Step 3: Enrol

When I say enrol, I'm not referring to signing a piece of paper or registering for a program. I'm talking about getting enrolled in the idea of something that leaves your client feeling inspired, motivated, enthusiastic, energised, and excited.

What your clients are enrolling in is a future they want but don't have right now.

You want to have a conversation that draws all of that out, gets them in touch with it, and naturally begins to enrol them into the idea they can have it ...

They become enrolled in the idea that it's possible for them to make it work ...

And they become enrolled in the idea that you can be the person who helps them make the dream a reality.

Take your clients on a journey to get them in touch with what they want more than anything else in relation to the specific area you help people with.

If it's business, what's the business of their dreams?

Health? What does healthy living look like, and why do they want that?

If it's about their relationship, what's the thing that they would love to have more than anything else in their existing relationship, or what kind of relationship do they want?

Our role is to help people get in touch with this thing they've been fantasising about, get them excited about moving towards it, and get them believing in the idea that we can help them and that what they want is possible.

Context for the conversation

Let me share a context I've had within every conversation I've ever had in my coaching business, and how I recommend all of my clients show up in their own calls.

I offered it earlier and want to offer it again. Here it comes . . . this call could be the most important conversation of your client's life.

That's how it is for me. I show up from that space, and that gives me enormous power. I stand for the difference I want to make in my client's life. They're talking to you because of something they want that they don't have. They're there because they're stuck with some aspect of their life, or they're doing well but want to go even further — either way, they want to see a difference in that area. They're open and willing, and it's our job to make the most of that opportunity. I show up from that place, relaxed, not being significant, but I am very intentional about this, and I recommend that you are too.

How to have the enrolment call

Let's look at what an enrolment call is. Call it whatever you like, but it's essentially a coaching conversation. It can be in person or else on a Zoom call. I recommend video over a traditional phone call, as videoconferencing creates a higher level of trust, safety, and connection that an audio-only phone call can never match.

We know they're there because of the challenge you and they already spoke about in the previous conversation, and you know they're open to having a breakthrough. We now need to get clear on exactly where they're at and what's really getting in their way. We want to dig deep and help your client share more about their challenge, how it's showing up in their life, and how it makes them feel. We want to revisit this and give it more space and time in the call.

This is where you get to do your thing and bring all your training, experience, and magical gifts, in all your uniqueness — so trust that you have got this. Here are some additional things for you to think about as you develop your skills around having powerful coaching conversations with your clients.

What's Happening Now

- Get a better sense of where your client is and what they're up against.

- Get curious about the results they have been creating.

- Help them see whatever it is that they are doing or not doing that's slowing them down.

How It's All Impacting Them

- Go deep into the emotional and physical impact of their challenge and what it's taking from them.

- From time to time, check in and see where they are.

Lean In

- Ask powerful, challenging questions, and be there as a coach.

- Dig in to what's going to make the biggest difference.

- You can only do that by understanding what's at the source of their challenges.

For me, the source of everybody's challenge is almost always a combination of two things: the things they are doing or not doing (their strategy), and the limiting conversations they are having with themselves that are simply untrue. You want to get to the bottom of all of that and help them start to see themselves and the way they are holding themselves back through what they are thinking and saying. That will expose what I call the 'No wonder!'

Powerful Questions:

- What belief must you have about yourself to be getting the results that you've ended up with?

- What are some of the strategies (things you have done or not done) you have been applying that have created these undesired outcomes?

When there are negative thoughts and emotions in control, we end up stuck with limited results. Even in cases where someone is pushing through their internal limits and creating results anyway, which happens all the time, their achievements won't necessarily satisfy them, because the underlying belief remains limiting and negative.

That's why many very successful people experience depression when they wake up one day and ask, 'Is this it?' For many, this becomes a life-changing breakdown that leads them to look within and live their life in a more spiritual way and in alignment with what's truly important.

Express all of your coaching process, methods, and training in your enrolment calls. Offer value, insight, reflections, more effective strategic ideas, and for deeper coaching, ensure you're getting to the heart of what they've been believing about themselves and the world around them. Help them get to the realisations like:

- No wonder I'm in this position!

- No wonder I've been feeling so frustrated!

- No wonder this has been going on for five years!

- No wonder things didn't work out between us.

- No wonder I'm broke!

- This is all starting to make a lot more sense.

Powerful Question: 'What Is This All Reminding You Of?'

This single question alone, when asked at the right time and in the right way, with a deep enough understanding of why we're asking it, can open so much up for a person and begin their intense healing and transformation.

Why?

So much of what we experience, attract, and generate in our life right now is an unconscious pattern. Childhood experiences, trauma, significant memories, decisions that were made, things we are still holding onto — the past.

We replay these scenarios over and over in our minds because our reptilian brain, which doesn't understand the concept of past/present/future, is stuck there, reliving it over and over.

And there is a higher design. To heal. We will find ourselves in patterns from the past until we are aware of it and where it's coming from, what it's reminding us of, and what there is to learn, grow through, and heal. Until then, human beings will keep banging their heads against the wall. Life's a fascinating journey of pain, suffering, and transformation through the pain and suffering. We need the pain and suffering to wake up. It's all perfect. Not easy! But perfect.

So we unconsciously manifest experiences and relationships that remind us of the past with a higher purpose — to bring our awareness to our patterns, heal them, and break free from them once and for all.

Powerful Question: 'Where Is All This Taking You If Nothing Changes?'

Once we have explored enough about the past and present, it's very powerful to open a window into the future for our clients based on the past and on the present situation.

This can feel a bit edgy for some clients. Nobody wants to open themselves up to the uncomfortable future they are heading towards. It's scary and confronting, but with your loving support, they'll feel clear and safe enough to look. This will help create a bit more motivation to not end up there: a wake-up call — and that's the intention of this question.

If someone hasn't had enough pain yet, and is not aware or awake enough yet, they will continue banging their head against the proverbial wall until one day when they've simply had enough. People are ready when they are ready and not a minute before. We exist only to help ready our clients, but we can't be ready for them.

Giving Even More Value

Once you have helped your client get a better sense of where they are and how they've ended up there, it's time to offer them even more value. This can be in the form of nuggets of wisdom, all the way through to a much deeper Breakthrough Process you have designed for them, or a combination of both.

What we're doing here is setting your call up in such a way that no matter what, your client is served, and they can leave having experienced real value by being with you.

We're also giving them a powerful experience that leaves them no longer wondering what coaching is or what it's like to work with you; they're having it right now and it's real, undeniable, and impactful.

The degree to which you can impact your clients' life in the time you have together will be directly related to the number of clients who want to work with you and who will go on to do whatever it takes to do that — because they'll finally understand and get the real value of working with you and the real value of coaching — it's priceless.

This is called enrolment.

Creating an Inspiring Vision

Powerful Question: 'Allow Yourself to Imagine as Big and as Bold as You Can. What Do You Really Want in This Area of Your Life?'

You want to go deeper into that vision and have it be so big and bright that your clients are left completely enrolled in it — excited and inspired. You also want to help them stretch, so listen to see if the vision is big enough. Are you also excited? Are you feeling inspired by them and their vision? If not, then trust yourself, say what's there for you to be said, and lean in ...

Another way you can frame their vision is by asking questions like, 'What if you stretch that vision by 10? What kind of vision would make your palms sweaty? What kind of vision would get you jumping up and down right now at the idea of having it?' 'If you could have absolutely anything, what would it be?' 'Tell me more ...'

These are questions we ask to help our clients get out of their heads and push beyond their mental limitations. Those questions will give them inspiration, energy, and so much power — all the things required to move through whatever obstacles are coming their way.

I remember a time that I had a client share her vision. She sounded happy, but I didn't feel she was in touch with her real vision. I said to her, 'I'm getting the sense this is NOT it. I'm getting the sense there's MORE and you're holding back. If you stopped holding back and gave yourself permission to dream big and go for what you want most in this world, tell me, what is it you really, really want?'

The key word here is 'permission'. Some people need permission to go for it, overriding the idea that they don't deserve their dream or that they can't have it. They do, and they can!

I could see the wheels turning for her. Then she looked at me and said, 'Ryan, I feel a little embarrassed to say this and I've never shared it with anyone but it's time to get this out — I want to be on *Mindvalley*!' Everything changed in the way she showed up. So empowered, almost relieved she'd said it, and absolutely lit up. That's when I *knew* that was it.

So, this is a great example of what it's like to stretch somebody's vision until something pops because you'll know it when you see it. Once you feel that sense of enrolment — and you WILL feel it — it's time to consider making your offer.

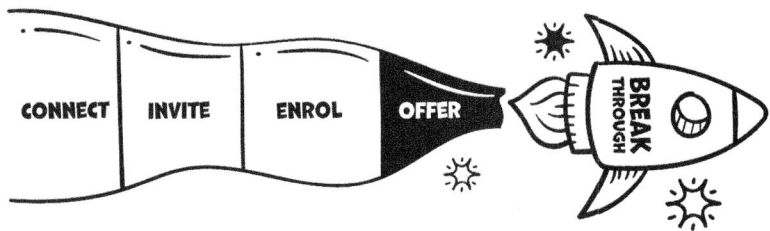

Breakthrough Process, Step 4: Offer

We've got to get our clients enrolled in their vision of the future so they're pulling the conversation towards them. When you're happy, your client's got a goosebump or two, and you're excited as well, you can make the offer.

We never offer our services if our clients aren't enrolled enough in their vision. If they're not enrolled enough in their vision, they won't work with you. Then you end up in an awkward place — convincing, twisting arms, and selling because your client is not pulling it towards them. They aren't enrolled.

When making your offer, you have two options:

1. Go into the offer right there and then, if it feels good for you both and time permits.

2. Schedule a follow-up call in two or three days (ideally no longer, because enrolment has a shelf life as the mind and life start to take over again), and on that next call, you can go through the offer.

Play around with it and discover what works best for you. When making the offer, we want to share the offer in a way that is simple, clear, and high-level. We don't want to get into too much detail because people can't handle too much information, especially if you are offering on the same call.

We do this through a process called PDOI.

- Process
- Delivery
- Outcomes
- Investment

We've covered how to create, develop, and bring all this to life in the previous chapters, and it all comes together as you make your offer. Share your process, how you deliver your process, the outcomes that are possible, and the investment required to achieve these kinds of results.

Breakthrough Process, Step 5: Breakthrough

Let's recap as we move into the last, final, and for a significant amount of your calls, the most important aspect of creating a high-fee client building your business and truly becoming an HPC.

- You've begun to develop Unshakeable Belief in yourself, your clients, and your business.

- You've laid all the foundations to enable you to move on and start getting you and your message out there.

- You've been connecting, inviting, scheduling calls, enrolling, and offering your high-fee program.

To get to this point really takes something, so well done! Take a moment and see how you have grown and how every single thing you confronted, developed, and broke through prepared you for the final step: the money conversation!

'The money conversation.' I say that this is where the real conversation starts and where we really get to show up powerfully as coaches for our clients.

For many coaches, this is the part that brings the most fear and anxiety, but it's beyond vital that you understand what's actually taking place here and how to lead it. If you can't talk about money, you're blocking the pathway to you and your clients getting what you both want.

This final piece of the Breakthrough Process — and the most important pillar to your business — is the actual breakthrough where clients pay you — yes, that's right. This is it!

It can happen that you make your offer, and your client is ready and happy to proceed right there and then — this is great and should be celebrated! It means you did a great job in the entire process so far and they were absolutely ready and willing to take the next step.

However, quite often, you may be met with some resistance no matter how well it seemed to go before. This resistance is grounded in a fear — the kind of fear that's been holding your clients back their whole lives — and it's going to take a bit more to help them break through it.

You must know that the beauty and power of being a High-Performing Coach is not about finding people who were going to say yes anyway. It's thrilling to hear yes after we say our fees!

However, there are others who are not quite there yet but present perfect opportunities. A wonderful client who really wants something and who is shown a pathway to having it but says no is on the verge of having the breakthrough of their life.

And there you are, in the business of helping people have the breakthroughs of their life. What could be more perfect?

We are now in a position to help our clients break through lifelong and ancient patterns. Now is the time to take their vision and turn it into a reality, kickstarting the biggest transformation of their lives.

In your calls, there will be breakthroughs throughout. However, the breakthrough we are referring to here is the type that shifts clients from, 'There's just no way I can do this', or 'I can't afford you', or 'I'll think about it', or 'I need to discuss this with my wife' to 'YES, I'M IN! How can I pay you?' This breakthrough means having them committed to the life they said they wanted in spite of their fears, doubt, patterns, and all their evidence from the past.

Regardless, if they do or don't have THAT breakthrough and become a client, you can feel honoured knowing that a difference was made, grateful for the opportunity to support someone in their life, and you learned how to fine-tune your coaching process. From a personal point of view, it was fulfilling. From a professional point of view, it was rewarding. But if you don't learn how to empower your clients to say 'Yes', you'll be left playing the yes/no game, and that can be slow and frustrating and leaves a lot on the table in terms of the difference you can make and what it really means to be a High-Performing Coach, not to mention the impact on your business growth.

This is why we are committed to helping our clients break through. It represents a life-changing moment for them and an access to building the business of your dreams off the back of what it's really all about anyway — transformation.

We exist to empower clients to have breakthroughs. What more important breakthrough is there for them to have than saying yes to what they really want in their life and getting fully committed to having it?

The money conversation

On the occasions when you present your fees, and your clients are pulling back, stuck, or putting up reasons and excuses, they're in breakdown mode. How you move on and engage from this piece of the process is pivotal to how you will build your business.

Keep in mind that whenever you experience any resistance to clients saying yes, everything before that point in the conversation felt like a connection and developed trust — it even made a difference — but nothing much has really changed.

The money conversation is where the real conversation starts because now the situation is real, and it's time to show up and empower your clients to do the same. Their saying no is not about you not being good enough (that's YOUR belief). It's because they're not enrolled enough, you haven't delivered a big enough breakthrough yet, or they're simply not able to believe this can all go their way. It's time to go to work. Time to do the real coaching.

When you make your high-fee offer to your client, it exposes the truth about where they're at and what's been truly stopping them. All the breakthroughs that came before, everything that got discussed, was simply an insightful set-up to a real shift. Real shifts take the form of a shift in action. The money conversation makes everything real because suddenly they're being asked to do something, to get committed and take a bold action.

The truth is, your clients are scared. They're being asked to commit while they're experiencing a lack of belief and a huge amount of fear around failing and are concerned with what others will think about them. It's confronting and will drive up all sorts of reasons, excuses, and patterns, a powerless sense of indecisiveness, and a lack of freedom to tell the truth.

The money conversation serves to expose and drive up this truth, and it is our role to make that a safe process and help shine light on what's really going on. The truth is stirring at a deep, subconscious level, usually disrupting a limiting condition they've been brought up in.They've carried these ideas around for years and found ways to survive despite these limiting ideas about themselves, their lives, and what they can accomplish.

These beliefs show up on the surface as:

- 'I don't have the money.'

- 'I don't have the time.'

- 'I need to talk to my partner.'

- 'I can't come up with that kind of money.'

- 'It's not possible because I have a wedding coming up.'

- 'I will think about it.'

- 'Wow, this sounds amazing. Please send me some more information and I'll come back to you.'

It can also show up as denial, disappointment, resentment, blame, apathy, guilt, shame ... a whole bunch of ways, all of which are negative, limited, and disempowering — which is great! We're now exposing the truth. Keep going ...

This is where your clients are at, and all the money conversation has done is exposed that. It's exposed how your clients are living their life, and no wonder. No wonder they don't have their dream life. It's our job to help them see the 'No wonder', because right now they don't see it. They're too stuck in their own unconscious thoughts and stories — and the inexperienced coach will buy into the stories, believe them, feel sorry for them, enable them, and even agree with them.

This is because, at this level, you begin to show up on the same vibration as your client, meaning you are also dealing with and buying into their stories as you buy into your own. In this case, you have nowhere to go with your clients and nothing to offer them, and these calls end with nothing major changing and you left scratching your head.

If your clients start reflecting yourself back at yourself, you'll find yourself agreeing with them, playing nice, and then you'll both be stuck.

The inexperienced coach:

- Backs out when they should lean in

- Tries to get off that call as fast as humanly possible, just like your clients are doing, because it's way too confronting and overwhelming

- Offers sympathy, discounts, or more free sessions

- Says things to themself like, 'I didn't want to push', and tells themself their client is not ready (projection)

- Makes it all about them (masked as a concern for their client)

All this is part of the learning process, so don't worry.

If you're noticing a pattern on your calls and you recognise yourself in what I'm pointing out, consider that your clients are leaving your calls in your clearing.

On my calls, clients come in in all sorts of ways, and more often than not, leave in a very different way — with belief and a real commitment to their dreams.

How is this possible?

Because I have belief and a real commitment to mine, this is my clearing.

Clients leave coaching calls in the clearing of the coach. That's the power of a coaching conversation.

How can you find a way to help more clients have breakthroughs and say yes?

Look at how your clients typically leave your calls and ask yourself, 'Where am I doing that too?' And start a process of bringing your awareness that you too, are doing that, so you can stop doing that.

Are your clients procrastinating? Start doing things now.

Are they indecisive? Start making powerful decisions fast.

Do they need to ask other people for permission to go for what they want in life? Make sure you stop doing that and give yourself the permission. And go for it!

Are they using reasons and excuses to stop themselves? Take total responsibility for the results you have gotten and the ones that you want. Are they simply unwilling to invest? Believe you are worth it, believe it can be done, and you can do it. Invest in yourself without doubt and from a place of total trust and deservedness.

Are they unable to find a way to get committed? Make sure you ALWAYS find a way.

As you start to make the shifts within yourself, you'll begin to understand your clients, what they're bumping up against, and how to help them break through. You'll start to lean in, with skill, from your heart and with an Unshakeable Belief in your client.

You'll say things you've never said before; you'll speak a wisdom that touches the very depths of your clients' spirit.

You'll show up for them in a way that nobody has ever showed up for them before.

Your coaching will take a new and profound form that will leave people present to their own greatness as you become more present to your own. And as this starts to happen, people just can't stop what comes next, because what comes next is YES.

Yes to themselves, yes to their life, yes to they can, yes to they're worth it, yes to they can do it, yes to wanting what they want, and yes to going for it no matter what!

And the beauty of it all? It all starts with you saying yes to yourself ...

If you are saying no to life, your clients will say no to you, and you'll have little to offer them.

Start saying yes now — to yourself and to your life — and allow something that looks and feels like magic start to occur on your calls, with your clients, and in your coaching business.

And if after all that, they still say no, that's OK! They got all they could and were ready to get, a difference was made, and everyone moves on. It's perfect.

Mastering the breakthrough conversation

Since 2011 I have led thousands of enrolment conversations in one form or another. In my coaching business, I progressed from a strategy of having an initial 90-minute deep dive of nothing but coaching to a follow-up call where I'd make my offer to having a single 30- to 60-minute call to create high-paying clients.

In the beginning, I didn't have a website or any social media presence. All I had was my mobile phone, my network, my coach, my experience, and a willingness to believe.

With this number of calls, I quickly began to see patterns in how the conversations would go and how to have them be effective. Everything is building up to the moment you say your fees, and you get to learn to not make that a big deal by being there to serve them no matter what. The money conversation is where I roll up my sleeves, ready to do the real work of empowering my clients to have a breakthrough while being completely unattached to the outcome.

I want you to imagine that whatever happened before the moment you state your fees — the conversation before it — means almost nothing now. No matter how well the conversation went, no matter how many breakthroughs they had, it now means almost nothing. At the point where your fees are out in the open and on the table, your client is now confronting their deepest and darkest fears. They'll often end up stuck in the stories they've written for themselves, and it can be painful. Hold space for them, let them be where they are at, let go of any attachment, and meet your client where they are in conversation.

You want to lean in and bring the best of what you have. I want you to imagine that you're leaning into the money conversation so far that if you leaned in one more millimetre, your chair would break.

The real magic ingredient here is the idea that to help your client shift from 'no way' to 'let's do this', you've got to shift their belief. What's showing up with your clients is a function of what they're believing about themselves, and you've got to help them see that. Without digging deep into what's really at play, there's no opportunity for a breakthrough.

Remember that it's our beliefs that are shaping all our actions, thoughts, and feelings.

So, resistance, excuses, reasons, deferring, and procrastination are all just the tip of the iceberg, covering up a set of conversations your clients are having with themselves. What are those conversations? They are, at this point, completely hidden from our clients' view. It's time to ask questions that will shine the light.

As we expose what's going on in the background, by getting deeper, they start to realise the truth.

Here's a conversation I had with a client that will help you see how this can be done:

> Client: Wow, this all sounds great, but there's no way I could afford that and besides, it's just not the right time for me.
>
> Me: I get it, so you're telling me it sounds great but there is no way you can afford it and it's not the right time; is that where you are at?
>
> Client: Yes, that's exactly where I'm at.
>
> Me: Mind if I lean into this with you? I can see a real opportunity for an opening.

Client: Yes, OK.

Me: Well, first of all, it's completely normal that you are saying this now — in fact I'm not surprised at all — and it's perfect.

Client: Oh really? How so?

Me: You shared with me on this call how badly you wanted to make this change in your life, and you were very courageous in sharing how you often end up stuck, not getting what you want because of your fear. You also shared with me how you often put up barriers to moving forward and convince yourself to back away.

Client: Yes, that's right, I've been seeing more how this has been a lifelong pattern.

Me: Exactly, and what I want you to get is that's all that's happening right now. It's right here in this conversation. You're doing it right now. Can you see it?

Long pause ...

Client: Yes, I'm doing it right now, aren't I?

Me: Yes, and it's normal and exactly what this call is about — to help you see what you've always done that has not been working for you.

Client: OK, but how do I deal with it? I really can't afford it!

Me: Consider it's really not about the money, or the timing; all that's simply a smokescreen.

Client: OK.

Me: Are you open to having a breakthrough around this?

Client: Yes, badly, but I'm so nervous!

Me: I get it, and it's OK. Let me show you how you can break through this and then you can choose where you want to go from there. Are you ready?

Client: Ready!

Me: OK, so let's review this. You came on the call wanting to take your life in a new direction, you shared how you wanted to have your vision as soon as possible, you told me you believed I could help you, I laid out what it looks like and what it will require on your part, and then you started telling yourself you couldn't afford it; it's not the right time. That's what it looks like to talk yourself out of and away from what you want. Are you following me?

Client: Yes.

Me: So, let's go a bit deeper. My question to you is, what are you telling yourself in the background that had you go from "I want this as soon as possible" to "I can't afford it; it's not the right time"?

Client: Hmmm, I feel embarrassed to say, but it's true; it's not about the money, is it? I have some money; I even have a credit card I never used . . . I guess I'm telling myself I can't have it. What if I fail?!

Me: Exactly, tell me more.

Client: I'm telling myself that if I pay this amount of money, and it all goes wrong, then I'm going to be even worse off than before!

Me: Yes, keep going.

Client: And well, I just couldn't handle that so it's like, better to stay where I am at and just accept I can't have what I want.

Me: Bingo. And how does all that leave you feeling?

Client: Deflated, annoyed, angry! Sad, actually.

Me: Thank you. Now, if you carry on speaking to yourself like this, where do you see yourself in a year or two?

Client: Same place, no better, maybe worse off!

Me: If you allow yourself to get connected to your vision again, what would you need to tell yourself to be able to make that a reality?

Client: That I can do this! That I deserve this! That if I just gave myself a shot, things could start to change; it won't be easy, but I can learn and find a way!

Me: Now, if you spoke to me from this space, and this way of believing in yourself and your future, what would you be saying to me right now about the opportunity for us to get committed to this and start working together? And — just to say — I won't hold you to this, I just want you to see it.

Client: I'd be saying, "Let's do this!"

Me: And if you did that, what might happen next!?

Client: Well, I'd start learning, I'd start growing, I'd start seeing results!

Me: And what might happen after that?

Client: I reckon I could actually make my dreams come true!

Me: Me too! So, now all you have to do is choose. Choose to tell yourself it's all going to fail, or choose to tell yourself it's all going to work out. You get to choose to believe or not. Either way, it's up to you — it's always been that way. You just never realised this, and you never learned how to be the kind of person who can be, do, and have whatever she wants. And I can show you how, and it starts right here. By bringing awareness to what you tell yourself and making a more conscious choice about that. So, what do you choose?

Client: How can I pay you?!!

I've had this conversation go this way hundreds of times. In having conversations like this, we built a seven-figure coaching business in little over two years.

Those clients went on to transform their lives, their business, their relationships, their coaching, their clients' lives … The ripple effect I have personally created through having powerful conversations like this over and over again is nothing less than immeasurable. I'm proud, humbled, and more than anything, I am excited for you to be able to have conversations like this with your clients too.

To master the money conversation, create high-paying clients, and have people consistently break through to say yes, you lean into their resistance. Coach them at the level of their beliefs, shift their beliefs, and create a space for breakthrough after breakthrough after breakthrough.

Do this, and you'll create more high-paying clients, more impact, and build an incredible business. And you'll get to look in the mirror and, without doubt, you'll know who you are and what you're capable of, and you'll give it all away to each and every client who has the privilege of talking to you.

I've coached thousands of coaches to learn how to do the same, and in partnership, together we have made a significant change in the evolution of humanity, because this conversation goes way beyond creating a high-paying client; it's changing the levels of consciousness of our world.

As I said at the beginning of this book, this is way bigger than money — we are partners in transformation, and I am committed to that.

The real intention behind enrolment calls

Enrolment calls are NOT about getting more clients or the money. And yes, we are committed to them breaking through, but we cannot be attached to that — whether they do or not is completely out of our control; we can influence it greatly, as you have seen, but it still requires them to take action.

Hear me out …

There's a more powerful intention that's going to serve you and your client deeply — to enable your clients to have a choice. A conscious choice.

When they're caught up in their limits and stories, they're reacting to their past. It's possible your clients have never experienced free, conscious choice ever before. Consider that your real job on the enrolment call is to get to a point where they can choose freely and consciously to move powerfully into this new world or choose to stay where they are. Not everybody will say yes to a new world, and it's OK when they say no. Your job is to allow them that beautiful gift of choice: free and conscious choice.

When people have this kind of opportunity (choice) in front of them, a significant number of them find a way to move towards this new possibility and powerfully choose it — but not without powerful coaching.

In my experience, 70–90 percent of the time you're going to meet some kind of resistance when you first offer your fees. Fear and unconscious thinking. Why? That's the state of the world and that's the condition of being human, and this is why you are here — to help people see, confront, and break through that which stands in their way. Also, you are new. They haven't read your book or watched a thousand of your testimonials, which naturally leaves them feeling skeptical.

It's all a perfect opportunity to master your coaching and bring the gift of free and conscious choice to your clients without any attachment whatsoever. How wonderful is that?

Coaching is an art form. You are an artist; your clients are artists too, wanting to create something wonderful. Your coaching conversations are the oil and brush, and your clients' lives are the blank canvas. Help them paint a beautiful vision and empower them to step into that vision and bring it to life.

Time to Raise the Price

You might not have to lean in for every call, but be prepared. Some clients will be ready to go and willing to spend the money. Others will not. Many factors influence this, one of the greatest being your audience, another being your fees, and of course, your coaching.

Joanne had a 100 percent track record over her first twelve clients after we helped her Connect, Invite, Enrol, and Offer. She experienced no resistance for her high-fee offer of £1,500! Amazing stuff.

So, my response to her? **'Well done! Now you can increase your fees!'** That started her on the next phase — stretching her own worth even more!

If you have people saying yes all the time, it means you're doing incredibly well AND your fees are too low. It has become too easy to work with you, and too easy for your clients. They could, can, and want to jump higher, and that's the power of getting your fees right — it empowers your clients to have the kind of breakthrough that will set them up for life.

So, I want you to go and discover a point where you start to meet more resistance, which you're able to break through and find the sweet spot in your fees that enables incredible breakthroughs and allows you to work with fewer, higher-paying clients.

Remember, your fees are yours and yours alone; you simply need to find a number you feel really great about and that is a match for the value you bring. And look, if that's $500, that's OK! $1,500? Perfect! $10,000? Good for you! Check in with yourself and make sure your fees genuinely feel great and exciting for you, and if they do, those are your fees.

Kelly's Breakthrough

'After joining HPC, my mindset shifted. I was able to put into place the systems and strategies to create a consistent and sustainable business. I fell in love with coaching, and within six months of learning how to apply the Five Essentials, I transitioned out of my other business and into coaching full time. I absolutely love what I do and the people I help every day.'

Kelly's biggest breakthrough was realising she had a gift to give to the world and knowing that, as a relationships coach, she could help her clients because she'd walked thousands of miles in their shoes personally.

'Becoming a High-Performing Coach taught me that it wasn't about the number of social media followers or having a massive PR presence. The greatest value I could bring was my own personal experience, combined with my skills as a certified coach. They tell you that you first need to have it before you can give it away. Once I understood that, I realised I had a truly unique experience and that if I was willing to be vulnerable and share that insight and knowledge, I could make a big impact on the world. Once that shift happened, I had more clients wanting to work with me than I could manage.'

Unshakeable Belief was key to getting Kelly started. 'Without it, I don't think I would have been willing to put myself out there like I do.'

She also found that the Breakthrough Process had a huge impact on clients, 'whether they decide to work with you or not. I have many clients who initially said no to working with me and came back later saying I'd made such a difference in their lives, and they were able to find the money to invest in themselves. Thanks to learning how to handle the money conversation, my conversion rate is above 50 percent and, like Ryan says, I'm rolling up my sleeves when I hear the concerns about the money — it's actually now my favourite part of the call!

'Over recent months I have gone from being fully booked with private coaching clients to creating a high-fee signature group program and my one-to-one fees have tripled, which allows me to help many more people and make more income!

'I'm continually developing my program to give more value to my community and not only to help singles find love but also to help them build safe, secure, and healthy families. If I could continue to expand on that, I would love to teach children the same skills and knowledge I am teaching singles, so they have the skills to select a compatible partner and build a healthy, loving, and secure relationship. It would be amazing to have an impact with children, so they don't have to go through the pain and suffering associated with divorce.'

Today, Kelly runs a successful high-fee online coaching business with one-to-one and groups and is also enjoying the challenge of expanding her team and scaling her business to reach even more people, while getting to do more of the part she really loves: coaching. She recently emailed me to celebrate her biggest month ever, which was more than ten times what she was earning before she integrated and applied the Five Essential Elements.

Exercise:
New Beliefs and Commitment

1. What new beliefs are you now creating about how you can show up on your enrolment calls?

2. What new beliefs are you now creating for how you can approach the money conversation?

3. What new commitment are you now making to yourself about how you show up in the face of your own barriers and breakdowns?

Go to www.ryanmathie.com/book and access my training on the Breakthrough Process to deepen your understanding even more.

8
Online Influence

*It's your time to shine like the bright
beaming light that you are.*

Gotta Show Up

Before working with HPC, Gabriela was receiving one inquiry
a month for her coaching abilities through her online content
strategy. She shared about how she would constantly feel

powerless when it came to growing her online coaching business.

'I wanted to start a group program that changed the way writers and creatives approached their work and careers, but I didn't know where to start. I was afraid that I would build it, and no one would come. I had a sense that success was something that happened to other people and that there was something wrong with me that I would never be able to fix. I would often feel envious when I met other coaches who had regular inquiries, and this envy would leave me feeling like I didn't deserve to work in personal development because I was a bad person.'

Gabriela was challenged around her beliefs about herself, and this was having an effect on her entire business, including how she showed up out there online.

Essential Element 4: Online Influence

Clearing the space for Online Influence

There was a time when having Online Influence was optional for a coach, but that was a long time ago.

Online is the space where people find out about you and get connected to you, who you really are, and the difference you are making. Online is where you can consistently share your wisdom, insight, experience, and magic. This is where you get to express yourself and share value with the world. The more that you do this, the more your audience will grow too. Even if you do nothing other than generate great content, your audience will grow and people will start to engage, reach out, and become clients.

See online content as the modern take on the published book. It might not have the same kudos, but it certainly has the same reach, if not more!

A caveat before we continue this section — I am not a marketing expert; marketing is not my passion, or I would be. I love the depth and the transformation, doing the work, and helping others do the same. This is why I have a team of incredible marketing experts around me at HPC and why I built this kind of team when I was ready to do that. However, after building multiple successful businesses, I have picked up a thing or two. The social media landscape is a fast-paced, ever-evolving space of new, exciting, and effective ways to connect. Facebook, LinkedIn, Instagram, and TikTok are the big ones at time of publishing, and there will always be the next new one. You'll want to stay open to exploring the opportunity of social media and stay up-to-date and current with the best ways to use them. You can choose to follow the trends, predict them before they hit, or stick with the platforms you know — it's a choice you get to make.

My intention here is to ensure you understand the essential nature of being online and creating the influence in the first place, and to make sure there is nothing in your way to being free to show up and express yourself.

In this section, I will share some of my own unique insights as a fellow coach that will serve you, but before I do that, I want to address the elephant that may or may not be in the room right now: your apprehension about being online and showing up! Now that you're getting the importance of showing up, we need to clear away anything that's stopping you from doing it.

Before we clear away your obstacles, please allow me to clear up mine and tell you my dirty little secret that I have never shared before . . . I really resisted this one in the early days. I still do in many ways, even now! Before I started working on my coaching business, I had closed my Facebook account and enjoyed a life beyond social media, notifications, and all the noise.

To learn to embrace and make peace with and even learn to love social media is an ongoing process for me.

Why am I telling you this? Some people love social media, and they naturally enjoy it. I am not one of them. I love coaching and I just want to coach!

So, if you're like me, and it's not really your jam, I want you to know that if I can find a way to make it work, then you can too! And it'll be well worth it.

My issue was never really fear; it was just about what I like/don't like. However, if you recognise that you are fearful or stuck around showing up online, let's dive into that, but if you're not in that position, you can skip this part and jump to the next section.

If you are feeling stuck, confronted, slowed down, or stopped in any way around going public, creating content, sharing yourself, or going 'live', whatever the resistance, by now I trust you have a better sense of where the resistance is coming from — the conversation you are having with yourself about yourself, and the conversation you are having with yourself about what others will think or say about you.

- 'I'm not gonna get it right.'

- 'I'm going to look stupid.'

- 'People will think I'm a fraud.'

- 'I don't know what to talk about.'

- 'I don't have anything good enough to offer.'

- 'I'm not as good as XXX.'

- 'I'll start showing up online when I'm more ready.'

- 'I need more training first.'

- 'I'm not good enough to be an Online Influence.'

- 'My content doesn't get much traction, likes, or comments, so what's the point?'

With regards to showing up online, take a moment now and write down what you are telling yourself about yourself, and what you are telling yourself about what 'they' will say about you, and bring a sense of presence to all that.

- Can you let that conversation be there and not make yourself wrong for any of that?

  Yes   No

- Can you give yourself some grace for all that's showing up?

  Yes   No

- Can you let it all go?

  Yes   No

- Can you create a more empowering conversation for yourself instead?

  Yes   No

  - Note: If yes, write new empowering conversation down now.

If you answered yes to all those, well done and good for you — you're ready to create Online Influence.

If you answered no to some, that's OK too — you might want to come back to this experience when you feel more ready or just push through it and take bold action anyway.

In either case, let's move on to exploring the kinds of content that will support you as you venture online, and create more influence, impact, income, and results.

Mum's Struggles

A little while back, I had a personal insight that dramatically changed the nature of HPC's online content strategy online. It happened with the most unlikely person: my mum.

She had developed a rash that had spread over about 40 percent of her body. She had seen a multitude of doctors and skin specialists and had test after test, but nothing had changed.

I was so concerned because I could see how it was impacting her. I introduced her to one of my clients, AJ, a brilliant and experienced health coach, who helped her get in touch with a probable allergy to gluten and dairy.

Given her age, she'd been eating a certain way for a long time, making it hard to change lifelong habits. At the same time, I was going through a major diet transition myself — eating mostly plant-based foods — and I was enjoying cooking. I'd been suggesting to my mum, 'Hey, just buy a cookbook that's exciting and get yourself into cooking some new plant-based foods, like me.' I even bought her a few cookbooks, and nothing really changed.

One fateful morning, I posted a beautiful picture on Facebook of a yogurt bowl with fruit and granola, and like all FB food pics, I made it look tempting. It got a huge response, and that's when it hit me!

What was going to change my mum's view on cooking food that was better for her had to be done in reality — not just by talking about it. She needed to see it for real. Now, I was in London at the time, and she was up in Scotland, so options were limited. The best thing I could do was take pictures and send them to her.

She loved them and would ask for the ingredient lists. Before long, she had a breakthrough. By cooking these pretty meals herself, **she experienced something instead of just talking about it.**

For many of us, talking is too conceptual. To have a real shift in beliefs, my mum needed to be able to experience something new. I needed to inspire her from a distance. The visual representation left her excited and shifted her beliefs around what her diet could be. It didn't shift with one picture; I sent her a few! With consistency and the passion to make a difference — I enrolled her!

Even better, within about six months of sticking to her new diet, the rash had completely disappeared, never to return again.

Breakthrough!!

Not only did the Facebook picture of my yogurt bowl give me inspiration about what my mum needed, it also gave me a major insight into what our business needed too.

Until that point, HPC had been posting fairly traditional content: case studies, personal stories, and insights. It was everything all of us see online — and is still effective to this day — but I suddenly realised there was a missing ingredient.

We were still just 'talking' about it. Talking can only go so far before it reaches a limit in depth and reach. I am always open to discovering new, more effective ways.

As coaches, our limitation with potential clients is that we are not in a real conversation yet, which leaves many people in a place of skepticism.

I realised that what made a difference to my mum would make a difference to our clients too. Our audience had to *see, experience,* and *discover* our work for themselves — from the safe distance of their mobiles, laptops, and homes. I knew that sharing real coaching conversations I was having — letting people see the process and transformations with their own eyes — would have a profound impact and help them by settling their skepticism to one degree or another.

I called a meeting with the team and said: 'Here's what we're going to do ... record our events, record me working with people and coaching them to have a breakthrough, and share those recordings with our audience. This way people can get the coaching as observers and get real value, and then they can see for themselves whether this is for them or not.'

We created the events, workshops, and special bonus coaching calls with clients and asked for permission to record so we could share with our audience and pay it forward.

Real content from real coaching conversations.

We could feel the impact on our business almost overnight.

Before long, people were coming on our calls feeling like they already knew me and my team and couldn't wait to connect and work with us. It was a major strategic move. It was about helping people see what could be possible for them without pressure. Our business — which was going extremely well — started to take off on a whole other level. We would have long-form, deep coaching conversations that we used as content for those who really wanted 'more', or who wanted to binge on HPC. From that content we pulled out quotes, email inspiration, five-minute videos, and fifty-second, or even thirty-second clips. This is high-value content that can easily be repurposed.

Now it's up to you to see if you're ready to do something similar. But look, maybe you're not drawn to this like I was. Maybe you're not ready for it, and that's OK. The main question I have for you is, 'What's the content you WOULD LOVE TO MAKE?' That's really what I accidentally discovered. Sit with this one and let yourself get connected to what content style or styles would really light you up and let it move you into action. Let people see your gifts in action, relate to your clients' stories, and see themselves in you and your clients.

Doing this will make you a stronger, more confident coach and allow people to have their own breakthroughs just by observing your content. You'll also build more trust, and they'll be left wanting more. This one shift in your content strategy will change your entire business.

We share video, and you can share video too — or audio, if there are concerns around privacy.

We ask permission from our clients at our online events to share some of the material if we believe it could serve people. The context for these requests? To partner with us in making an even bigger difference — 99 percent of people we ask are happy (in some cases, thrilled) to be involved and generously share their struggles and breakthroughs for a purpose much bigger than themselves. Seriously inspiring!

Content That Connects

Your content must reflect your journey and be authentic, transparent, vulnerable, and real — so it connects to your larger audience. Too many coaches think they have to present themselves as superhuman.

However, many potential clients find it hard to connect with superheroes because they're not real. People connect with real people. They're going to relate to your struggles, challenges, and the truth. If you're being inauthentic, your ideal clients will feel it on a deeper level and not feel drawn to you. Your authenticity will build deep connection, pull people towards you, and enable you to build your business.

I read a quote recently that said something like, 'Show people your scars, so they can believe they can heal.' I don't know who wrote it, but I loved it because it represented my own views of being vulnerable and sharing; that's why I had such willingness to share myself since that day back in 2009.

People are more likely to be real and open with you because you show up as real and open to them — you create a safe space to be human — and for a coach this is golden. You don't have to be anything other than yourself. Share your stories, be open and transparent. Talk about your struggles, your truth, and what it took you to break through. Paint a picture of the whole process, what you went through, and how you did it versus constantly telling people what to do. It's about balance. Sometimes it's great to give direct and clear ideas; sometimes a more humbled approach works best. Maintain a healthy balance in your approach, play around with ideas, and open yourself up. People will be enrolled in you and inspired to act.

Your ideal clients will follow you and want to build a relationship because they'll feel that if you can do it, maybe they can as well.

That's the real true purpose behind your content. Assuring people that they're not 'the only ones' going through it, leaving them inspired that they can also do what they want to do, whatever that may be.

Your content wants to address the reality that even though it's hard, and it's challenging, your audience can break through and create whatever life they want. Use real-life examples when creating content.

Some of the most enriching and powerful questions to ask are, what were your biggest challenges that you have broken through? What did you learn from it all? What are the insights? What is it that you've got to share with anybody else going through that?

Breakdown/Breakthroughs content

Raw and vulnerable content is inspiring. People connect with your authenticity. Another great place for content is from the coaching conversations you're having with your clients. Every conversation that you're having with somebody is going to show you something about what people are dealing with. There's a pattern you're seeing, and you can turn those observations into content.

A client once said to me, 'Do you know, I just wish I had simple steps to build a £10K a month business.' He was struggling with how to take those steps. I used that comment to go and do a piece on LinkedIn the very same day: *Here's how you build a £10K+-per-month Coaching Business in 9 Steps.* It was simple and clean, and it trended on LinkedIn. To this day, people are still commenting on it.

Go to www.ryanmathie.com/book and access this post online.

Your clients teach you everything you need to know about yourself, your business, and your other clients and what they are dealing with. They are a mirror to the human experience.

The more we can share our insights with others, the more people are going to benefit.

Bold and direct

Another practical way to create content is by creating simple yet transparent posts.

Remember this example: *Hey, I'm practising my coaching calls, and I would love to know if anybody would like to have a free session.*

I'm never surprised at how many people can create an extraordinary number of powerful conversations, make a difference, and learn on both sides with these kinds of approaches from time to time. If you're applying the Breakthrough Process, and fostering powerful conversations, what will happen at the end of the conversation is that your practice clients often start asking you, 'How do we do this again? How can I work with you?'

Another bold example is something like the following: *I'm looking for five ambitious women who are ready to claim their power, take a stand for themselves, and change their lives for good. If that's you, take the first and most important next step by sending me a DM now. I can't wait to hear what you're up to!*

Many of our clients have experienced great responses from such posts. They're almost always the ones who were already out there sharing valuable content, inspiring people with their willingness to show up, and doing so with consistency and heart.

Lead with value

You could be sharing your free workshops or webinars or sharing the inspiring community that you are building.

However, lead with value first, versus the call to action. Always give before you ask. Remember, it's the value you bring and the difference you make that draws people to you and leaves them feeling grateful for the experience. Lead with value, and people will naturally be more interested and open to wanting to continue the conversation. Take on your content game from the perspective of Social Serving vs. Social Selling, and you'll discover a very natural, potent, effective, and creative process with your content creation.

I have found content that leads with ...

value,

value,

value,

and ends with a

"P.S. Call to action ..."

Client interviews

Client interviews make great content. This is not the same as client testimonials, although such an interview becomes a testimonial too. In the coaching world, there is almost nothing more magical and enrolling than sharing a real, live, and raw conversation with a client whom you have worked with, who's been there, went through the pain, took your coaching, and created breakthroughs in their life to such a degree that they are now standing in the spotlight, able to share the whole thing.

Your audience will be watching; they'll see themselves in your clients' journey, and they'll be left feeling more trust in you and your work — as well as with a very simple and powerful idea that could change their life: 'If they can do it, then so can I.'

In your interview, put your clients up front and centre, thank them, acknowledge them, be in awe of them — for they are the true heroes, and heroes are real. Interviews also create so many opportunities for repurposing to shorter posts and clips — so much gold!

Book your first client interview today! This is how we do it — real, raw, and fun. Go to www.ryanmathie.com/book and watch our HPC interviews and feel yourself inspired in all sorts of ways.

Building a community

Many of our clients have enjoyed incredible success building their own community.

Communities are a great place to build your audience and widen your network. Then that community becomes your house. That becomes the place where you get to express yourself. And people love communities.

HPC has also enjoyed great success building our own Facebook community, How to Attract More Committed Clients. It's a great place to share more value and build connections.

We started with one person in the community, and through sharing it consistently, at time of writing we now have more than 12,000 members (and it's growing every day).

Building your own community is no different than building your own stage. With a clear name, people will feel drawn to your community and will want to be part of it.

You then get to show up and serve the people who want solutions to the problems you are helping people overcome.

If you have your Business Foundations set and clear, it could be time to start your own community too!

Be consistent

Consistency in how you show up online is key. People respond well to consistency. If you're posting randomly — some weeks you post nothing, other weeks you've got a big rush — you'll lose people's trust and confidence. People stalk and want to verify you, see if you're the Real Deal. If they see you're posting content, but nothing's been posted for four months, you might lose them. Or if you're showing up one way on Facebook, but completely differently on LinkedIn, that'll break trust as well.

Also, pay attention to your profile information and bios. Make sure they are clear versus clever, and consistent across all platforms. Make it obvious at first glance who you are, what you are up to, who you help, and how you help them.

Start conversations

If you want to launch, build, and grow with velocity, you must be starting conversations with all those people already in your network, and dedicating time each day to doing so. I recommend an hour a day minimum. Your content is reaching more people because there are many different ways social media will go beyond your existing network — and starting conversations will help widen it.

Remember, there's your organic endeavour to manually search social media and connect with people you feel drawn to. Connect with freedom and space around you. Be open. Don't make any decisions about anyone as you continue to learn and refine your understanding of your audience. Be a bright beaming light of intentional possibility.

If people like your content, comment back. Start a conversation, or maybe take the conversation private by direct message. Take some time to review their profile, and comment on their content too — take a genuine interest. Some people have one online social media strategy in that sense. They spend a few days only commenting on other people's content and creating a connection in that way. At some point, that person starts to look at what you're doing, starts a conversation, and off we go! That's just another simple way you could think about doing this.

Trust your intuition

One of my female clients shared with me that starting conversations just didn't feel right for her. She shared with me that she much preferred showing up and creating great content instead, and that each time she did that, she created connections, requests, comments, and inbound inquiries. I could tell in her voice she was a little scared to tell me this, so she was completely shocked by my response.

I said to her, 'You have what I call the Flower Power Strategy. Like a flower, you open up and bloom, spreading your beauty and sweet essence, and all the bees come to you.

'This is your feminine essence and energy. Trust in it, play with it, go with it, and keep doing what works for you. One thing to bear in mind with the Flower Power Strategy: flowers come out and up every day with the sunshine, so you want to show up as much as you can with this approach — ideally every single day, at least Monday to Friday.'

She was so relieved to hear this, and she acknowledged that she simply needed that permission from me, and that for her, creating content is like flirting and way more aligned and fun for her, not to mention effective! I said, 'Flirt away!' We both laughed, and off she went to charm the world with her divine feminine wisdom and beauty.

Energy is very important; many of the strategies laid out here are grounded in the masculine (I'm a man, after all) and much is grounded in the feminine too (I've done a lot of work to integrate a healthy balance of both conscious masculine and feminine energy). We need a balance of both, not only to build this business, but to live an extraordinary life!

So keep all that in mind, listen to your instinct, let yourself try new things, and trust the process.

Frequency

How often and when should you post?

There is SO much different data on this. Your best bet is to Google it and see what's current, because the goalposts tend to move a bit. You might not need to necessarily post every single day, but you can if you want. More is more! On the major platforms, I wouldn't post *less* than twice a week, but every platform is a different environment. Allow yourself to be influenced by the environment itself and play the game.

On LinkedIn, I post written content twice every week — because that works for me. I post two Lives across all my socials using Stream Yard (a tool that allows you to simultaneously post across your platforms at once) every week. If you feel good about posting more, post more. If you prefer to post less, perhaps start with once a week and go from there. See what feels good and what works for you; the main thing is that it is a regular flow and you're showing up!

A Context Reframe on How to Approach Social Media Forever

After helping thousands of coaches build and refine their online presence and strategy, it became clear to me that people were having so many blocks around social media and were unable to show up freely. It occurred to me they just needed a more powerful context to help them do that.

So I started to invite our team and our clients to see social media as one big, online, on-demand networking event. At networking events you mingle, say hi to people, start conversations, and get connected. So often new opportunities arise from a multitude of interactions: new clients, new collaborations and partnerships, insights and ideas, referrals, and invitations to podcasts. You name it — anything is possible through connecting and having conversations. How often would you go to a networking event? How often would you like to? How hungry are you to make an impact? How much time and energy are you willing, able, and ready to invest?

I encourage you to start seeing the online space exactly how you would an in-person networking event. If someone likes your post, like theirs back and start a conversation. If someone comments, respond to that comment and let things flow, add those people as friends/new connections, and start a private conversation. Connect and see what opens up.

Some people you connect with won't want to take it further, and that's OK. However, many people would love to connect and be open to taking it further. Many would love to become a client. You simply need to connect, invite, and follow the Breakthrough Process.

I'm never surprised at the magic that can happen when two powerful people get connected. Start connecting right now and keep connecting. Watch how your business will flourish in life-changing ways!

Allow yourself to think about the online space as one big networking event. It's a fully interactive, on-demand networking event. You're out there to connect with people for real, and to see what opportunities can open up.

Choosing to see social media in a negative way, or something you have to do — this only gets in your way. You don't have to show up online, but it's going to make a tremendous difference if you do. There are personal breakthroughs to be had and influence to be made. Once you naturally start being yourself, you're just going to start talking to people, being curious about them, and asking them what they're up to. You can ask them what they're looking to create or what their big focus is. Maybe you ask about their challenge … maybe you ask if they'd be open to having any help, if you think you can offer it. Being free to see people as people is how you show up online.

Gabs's Breakthrough

Gabs's main platform while working with HPC was YouTube. She was getting some results with her content, but the more she learned to connect with people and narrow down her niche, the more her channel began to grow. 'Now, when I take an inquiry from someone, they say things like they feel they know me because they've been binge-watching my videos. I had confidence as a performer and public speaker before HPC, but the cherry on top is that I now have confidence that what I do changes lives.

'HPC has given me the tools to create clients and impact people's lives powerfully. It also provided a model for how to run a community. This last point has been super valuable for me and has helped me to create my own loving, safe community — both within my coaching program and also in the public communities I run online. I find it so rewarding to know there are people eager to tune in to what I teach.

'I liked the simplicity of Unshakeable Belief, which meant that I could at least hold it as a phrase in my mind to aspire to (even though I knew I didn't have it).'

Anytime Gabs had a challenge — such as a potential client not showing up for an inquiry call (which was happening a lot in the early days) or receiving 'no' after making an offer to her coaching program, she would be able to say those words in her mind and ask what someone else who had this would do.

'I was able to eventually evolve into someone who genuinely FELT what Unshakeable Belief was. I learned how to talk to myself consciously. Often now, my clients will say that the reason they felt drawn to work with me was because of my Unshakeable Belief in them. This was something I discovered — when I learned to feel Unshakeable Belief in myself, it meant that I knew my coaching would be able to change lives.

'With this powerful framework of how to create clients and continue to grow, I know I can trust in the future I want to build with my life and career. I have been able to do what I help my clients with, which is build a business and write a book. I am enjoying the ability to create £10K month and the creative freedom this gives me — I can either step back for a few weeks and work on my writing or go again! This has meant that I have been able to finish a memoir, and I am now having exciting conversations with agents. It has also meant that I've had the time to continue to focus on my YouTube channel and begin to develop another dream to become a world-renowned interviewer. There is nothing like the feeling of having total independence to create exactly the career I want, knowing that I can continue to grow my business, generate the income that feels right, as well as continue to develop my own life and pursue creative goals.'

Today, Gabriela confidently helps writers and creative entrepreneurs make an impact and an income. She is a life coach, shamanic practitioner, and NLP practitioner.

Exercise:
New and Aligned Beliefs

- What new and aligned beliefs are starting to show up for you around being online?

- What new and aligned beliefs are starting to show up around the difference you can make by showing up more authentically online?

- What new strategy ideas do you feel ready to implement?

9
Accountability & Coaching

"This is the big one."

Andrea was a straight-A student at school and university. In her own words, she was the cockiest young woman you'd ever meet.

'I used to fully believe "There's nothing I can't do, only things I haven't learned yet," and I would pull this phrase out any time anyone told me I couldn't do something.'

That was all to change when her ex-husband took his life in 2012.

Andrea worked through so much personal grief and limits and was ready to make a difference. She came to us with zero business structure. Her previous business as a dominatrix had operated by her tweeting a pretty picture, throwing insults at a camera, and waiting for the phone to ring. 'I had no idea about planning, strategy, or how to show up online,' she said.

'Before I started working with HPC, I was an openly recovering alcoholic dominatrix trying really hard to be an NLPer, hypnotherapist, and/or coach. "And/or" is deliberate, as I was willing to take what I could get, as my studio had closed due to lockdown, and I had gone from a comfortable, easy lifestyle to a zero-income hell.

'I think it traumatised me, but I had no idea what trauma was. All I knew was my mind wouldn't do what I wanted it to do, and the more I tried, the worse it got. I resigned myself to being stupid for the rest of my life, and it took me to some dark places. I had zero self-belief for eight years, and getting sober was part of that healing process, but I felt like it wasn't enough. My ambition was starting to grow, but it was weighed down with fear and a crippling lack of trust in myself.

'I was full of doubt and fear, believing I had made a huge mistake by being so open about my recovery and being a domme, because who would listen to an alcoholic sex worker? I was generating zero but paying for Facebook ads (advised by the hypno trainer at the time) and getting nowhere ...

'My online approach before HPC was to post pretty pics and a clever line underneath. No one liked my pictures, never mind contacted me. I branded them, thinking I was clever but nope — not one bit. I did an Instagram Live and rambled about my sobriety journey for 30 minutes and connected with one woman who signed up for 10 sessions at £800, but I charged her £600 by accident and was too scared of breaking everything so I said nothing … I thought, *Beggars can't be choosers*. The future just looked very bleak, and I was hiding behind my domme persona and a fancy website, as I had zero faith in myself that I could make this happen.

'I learned to be a hypnotherapist in a group via Facebook Lives and a platform. I felt lost, though. I had no one to practise with, so I started a practise group on a Saturday and invited a few people along. We have become lifelong friends, but none of us had any clue about running a business or accountability.

'I'd also been a lone wolf for 18 years in a previous industry that could be quite isolating and lonely at times.'

Essential Element 5: Accountability & Coaching

The fifth and final Essential Element is Accountability & Coaching; this is where we get to be held responsible for the planning, organising, application, integration, training, development, and implementation of all the parts.

As powerful and as essential as each element before it, Accountability & Coaching is the most critical by nature, and in my experience, represents 80 percent of the whole because this is where it all comes together!

I'm a massive believer in the Pareto principle.

Otherwise known as the 80/20 rule — 80 percent of your results come from 20 percent of your efforts.

Having taken hundreds of coaches to six figures now, I can say this with certainty.

The 80/20 rule is as relevant today as it was back in the early 1900s when economist Vilfredo Pareto revealed 80 percent of the land in Italy was held by 20 percent of the people.

We see it in all walks of life now:

- 20 percent of criminals commit 80 percent of crimes.

- 20 percent of drivers cause 80 percent of all traffic accidents.

- 80 percent of pollution is pumped out from 20 percent of all factories.

- 20 percent of any company's products make up 80 percent of sales.

- 20 percent of employees produce 80 percent of the results.

Don't forget: 99 percent of the world's wealth is held by just 1 percent of the population. (Jeff Bezos, Bill Gates, and Elon Musk are just a few of those in the 1 percent).

Meanwhile, 80 percent of coaches fall into the low-income category (some as low as $0K–$2K/month), while the other 20 percent are more likely to earn in the high five figures, or six figures a year (some of those coaches much, much more!).

So how does 80/20 apply here?

Eighty percent of your results from the Five Essential Elements come from 20 percent of them (this one).

Eighty percent of your potential results from reading this book will come from 20 percent of the chapters (this one!).

It's through understanding that it's about being held accountable, and being trained, developed, coached, and supported to integrate all the ideas, break through the barriers, trained and developed, and to be who you said you wanted to be and to obtain the results you wanted to create that accounts for 80 percent of your results.

Many coaches know they need someone or something to keep them accountable, and of course they get the importance of coaching! However, many struggling coaches don't have this, as part of their structure right now or maybe they engage in some kind of accountability structure that is less effective. It is often said that something is better than nothing, but as a High-Performing Coach, it really is essential to be part of a high-performing Accountability & Coaching.

Your environment is a huge aspect of what is influencing your results. For example, if most of your kitchen is filled with junk food, guess what you will most likely be eating? You know that unhealthy food is bad for your energy, your mood, and your health. All of that is a function of your environment. Change the script, ditch the junk food, and replace it all with fresh fruits and vegetables. That's going to have a more positive effect on your diet, your mood, your health, your energy, and even your finances. The environment greatly impacts your habits, which greatly impact your results.

Accountability & Coaching for an HPC is about being part of an environment that will have a positive impact on your coaching business. Often, coaches are siloed away from the rest of the world. They're working alone, which can be lonely. When we're alone, most of us find it hard to push beyond the limits, and you'll never see your blind spots on your own — hence, the word 'blind'.

It's easier for us to get stuck and become ineffective. This becomes the norm for lots of coaches trying to figure out their business on their own.

The longer you stay a lone wolf, the less effective you are as a coach and business owner. After working with thousands of coaches, we know this is a common situation new coaches find themselves in. They tell us about the negative effects of working on their own and not being part of effective Accountability & Coaching.

It's also why — while offering books, videos, blogs, free content, and one-off coaching sessions or events are all hugely valuable — there is only so much that they can bring, because the real difference gets made over time, with support, guidance, and coaching around the next big breakdown, and being empowered to cause the next big breakthrough.

This is why you should never be concerned that you are giving too much away through your published content or on your enrolment calls; it's a fraction of what's possible when you are in a committed environment completely optimised for your results.

A common objection many coaches don't know how to handle is when they've led a really powerful call, the client says thanks and that they feel ready and confident now to go off and implement the changes, and the coach responds with a 'great!'.

Not great, and you know it.

Nothing major changes in an hour. It doesn't work like that. If you think it does, then you may well be disconnected from the true power of profound coaching or maybe you just never had deep and profound coaching.

When you are connected to the true nature of coaching, you would never say 'great' or be lost for words. You'd say, 'hold on ... It doesn't work like that!' and continue to educate, support, and coach your client towards what's going to serve them the best — maybe even call them out — so they could make a more informed and conscious choice about what's next for them.

So the next time you think about holding back on your calls, hold nothing back, give them everything you've got, and when they're lit up and completely present to the power of your coaching, ask them, 'If we've accomplished all this in an hour, imagine what we can accomplish in three months? Would you like to talk about that?'

How to Create Positive Accountability & Coaching

Casual Accountability & Coaching

Let's explore different types of Accountability & Coaching that can positively influence your performance. The first one is what I refer to as casual Accountability & Coaching. It's one you have with your friends. You may have an accountability call once a week and support each other. It's fun, free, and you can set it up quickly. The more transparent you can be with each other, the greater chance of success that Accountability & Coaching is going to have.

However, one of the downsides of casual Accountability & Coaching is there's no skin in the game, meaning there's not much to lose because there's not enough on the line. It's easier to play it safe. There's not as much urgency to create results. Another is that you're hanging out with someone on the same level. Nothing wrong with that, and it's a good start. But it's not the most efficient Accountability & Coaching to create major breakthrough results.

Focused Accountability & Coaching

This may be a friendly yet focused mastermind group, or weekly calls, with people you've met in previous programs or trainings. These groups are empowering, supportive, and particularly comforting in the sense that everybody's in the same boat and dealing with the same challenges. Again, there's still no skin in the game, and this lends itself to a lack of action.

The second major drawback, as with before, is that you're part of an accountability group with several people who are at the same level as you or a little bit ahead or behind. This carries the risk of becoming a case of the blind leading the blind. You'll get lots of agreement and feel supported; however, in the background, the results are diminishing because of the limited nature of what is available in this type of Accountability & Coaching. This kind of structure can work better if you're surrounded by high performers, but you'd have to be one, too, to get the invite, and you might not be there yet.

High-Performing Accountability & Coaching

Last, there's committed Accountability & Coaching, which is by far the most powerful. You're committed financially, emotionally, and mentally to the process. You and everyone around you are all in — that's powerful!

You're surrounded by and supported by experts who've done it all before and who are there in complete service of you. They're leading you down the path they know well, towards the results you want to create. This environment will give you the feeling you've got your feet held to the fire and you'll take more effective actions than ever before. You'll be held accountable, helped through any mental and emotional blocks, and supported in a way that's going to create more breakthroughs.

This is an environment that is intelligently designed by experts who know what it takes to create the results you want to create.

There's accountability, training, and ongoing development.

You can confidently surrender to the process laid out in this space, and all you have to do is show up, take the coaching, do the work, play full out, and you will see results.

I've tried all these environments and quickly learned the casual approach just didn't work for me. It wasn't committed enough. I needed to have that skin in the game. I wanted to be out of my comfort zone, learning from experts who had accomplished what I wanted to accomplish. While that focused environment was friendly and supportive, it wasn't powerful or effective enough for me either. I always found myself drawn to being in powerful, committed accountability structures because I knew that's where I was going to be challenged the most, and it's where I knew I thrive the most. It's one of the major reasons I built HPC with a team — I wanted to create my own high-performing Accountability & Coaching. This is next level! I always want the best and most effective options that are available for me. I encourage you to strive to have the same.

I shared with you earlier in this book that I dedicated a specific period of my life to my health and fitness. What sparked this off was two things: I had space and time to get in touch with what was important to me, which was my health. And I remember one day I took a good long look at myself and my body in the mirror — I was not in good shape. Normally, I'd suck in my stomach and move on, but this time I just stood there and looked. I confronted the reality of the shape of my body and that I was simply not taking care of it, and I said to myself, 'Enough is enough.'

So many of us have gotten to this 'enough is enough' stage, be it in our health, relationships, business, and so on … On this day, looking in the mirror, I called 'enough is enough' on my health and fitness. I downloaded a fitness app, paid my money, and I never looked back.

As my focus began to shift to my business in 2017, my fitness training became less and less a priority until it went completely out of existence in 2018.

For a few years, I had a number of false starts at getting my training back on track, but it never happened.

So on January 1, 2022, I made a decision which, as it is for so many of us, was fuelled by the possibility of a new year: 'Get yourself back on track by the end of January or hire a trainer and go all in.'

January came and went with little change, and on February 1, I walked into the gym, asked to speak to the most experienced trainer, and made a commitment to work with him three times a week on an ongoing basis.

He asked me my three main objectives, to which I replied, 'Other than to get strong and fit, my three main objectives are accountability, accountability, and accountability.' We both laughed.

In the first few weeks, the number of times I woke up with the thought of cancelling my 8:30 am session was hilarious to me. And every time I had the thought, I felt grateful for my PT and the structure I had created for myself; then I got my ass out of bed and into the gym. Now I that have the habit — the routine — the results are coming and it's all thanks to having a structure that works for me and my life.

I want you to consider bringing a similar intentionality to your coaching business. Our One Day Business Launch Pad (formerly known as One Day Intensive) is renowned amongst coaches the world over for breakthroughs, transformation, taking action, and creating results.

'I connected with more people today than I have since I started my coaching business!'

'I booked more calls today than I have in the last month!'

'I created a high-fee client just two days after the training!'

I hear it all the time ...

How is this possible? Powerful coaching, development, and accountability.

In our programs, our clients are in massive and consistent action. There are highs, lows, ups, downs, breakdowns, break-throughs, sorrow, joy, tears of disappointment, tears of joy ... It's all there, and it's all headed intentionally and deliberately in one direction — through each and every single barrier our clients come up against. They are inspired, motivated, guided, held, coached, empowered, and held accountable for their greatness. It's incredible to witness the determination of our clients and all the sweeter when, one by one, the results come for them. Incredible, remarkable, and astonishing results.

Results that were simply not going to happen any way but by being part of high-performing Accountability & Coaching and then showing up, being willing to do the work, being extraordinary coachable — things moving with velocity, and the possibilities in the space being palpable. Wow.

As you thrive inside Accountability & Coaching, you will not only create better results for your business, but you'll also have a deeper understanding of how to create Accountability & Coaching for your clients because this is something they need and will thrive in too. I'll never forget this one client who came to our free and one-day events for a year until one day I called her out in front of a live audience of 250+ coaches. I saw her on the corner of my screen, interrupted my agenda and said, 'Nina! Great to see you! When are you going to have a breakthrough and get in our program?' I coached her around her blocks — laid it all out there for her — and she finally had a breakthrough and came into our program. She absolutely transformed inside our environment and created about $10K in a matter of weeks (from never having created a paying client). I started calling her Ninja! When she finished the program I approached her, enrolled her, and the next day she joined us at HPC, and it's been a success story for us all ever since. Now she's our Breakthrough Director, a leading figure in our community, and a face of our business! What a turnaround!! That's the power of this most essential element, number 5.

Andrea's Breakthrough

Andrea felt like the lights came on when she started working with us.

'I was the first in my group to discover HPC, and I went back to my group, excitedly telling everyone I had signed up, and every time I signed a client everyone there became more curious and started to join workshops run by HPC. A few have now joined the community and have gone on to become High-Performing Coaches in their own right, which is cool as I get to see my buddies do well too. Community is everything. Fellowship is what got me sober, so that structure is vital to my success, and HPC has this in abundance.

'Everything I have been challenged to do I have thrown myself full-force into, and it has paid off in ways that money can't buy. Having someone in my corner, holding me to a higher standard than I did myself, made all the difference. That self-assured woman I had buried is back.

'Ryan asked us to set a game for the first 90 days. I said £15K, thinking if I got half of that I would be happy, but once it was out there, I got super single-minded, and I created this in two weeks. Spurred on by this, I kept going and went on to create £24K in the 90 days — limited only by the number of coaching hours I had left to offer. I was at capacity. My confidence and self-assurance were through the roof, and my only fear was more people saying yes and I couldn't take them on. This is why I decided to offer group coaching, but with no idea how to make this happen, I went to the experts, obviously.

'Life really could not be better, and I am exactly where I need to be as a coach, a businesswoman, and a human being. As Ryan says, we can only take our clients as far as we have gone ourselves. Working with HPC and applying all five of the Essential Elements has had such an incredible ripple effect on my clients because I am doing the work.'

Today, Andrea helps passionate women become unleashed, powerful, and in action everywhere in their life. She has been able to go much further than she ever dreamed because she found the right kind of accountability, coaching, and support.

10
The Real Deal

Time to walk your talk.

Before Rick started working with us, major world and economic changes were strangling his revenue, and he didn't know how to build the business.

He was discouraged and realised that unless he took immediate action, his business was in peril. Hearing the distinctions was a total shock.

'I was struck by the simple but powerful truth of "No conversations, no business" and "It can be done, and you can do it",' Rick says. 'It became very clear what action I needed to take.'

Rick was suffering a crisis of confidence, which shifted to the beginning of Unshakeable Belief, after I tasked him to talk to his previous clients to ask for testimonials. He was shocked how powerful they were, and it gave him enormous power. Believing more than ever in the power of their work, he began to understand that if a potential client were not open to having a conversation with them, that was OK, and they could move on.

For many years, he had enjoyed a clearly defined niche in the insurance distribution vertical, but he lacked a clearly defined high-fee/entry-level program. In one of their first sessions, I challenged Rick to create a program on the spot, right there, and he created the Passionate CEO program with a fee of $5,000. **He created his first high-paying client the very next day; talk about a quick turnaround!**

Today, Rick is a Business Coach and Consultant who helps ambitious entrepreneurs build great companies and achieve exceptional results through a seven-step process called Building a Passionate Enterprise. He and his team are growing more than they ever imagined because they incorporated all of the Essential Elements.

The Breakthrough Process gave Rick a clear track to run on when approaching a potential client. 'I have been in sales for many years, but having this simple step-by-step that wasn't "salesy" to follow dramatically increased my effectiveness and my enrolment success.'

Rick gained a solid connecting process that started yielding a consistent flow of new potential clients. He also committed to systematic publishing, creating a strong presence in his niche.

'In August, I was without direction, had an empty pipeline, and my revenue was dwindling. I began working with HPC in September and by year's end, I had put more than $100,000 in new revenue on the books!

'Me and my team started the New Year with a bang! In January, our new revenue exceeded $70,000, and our pipeline is robust. There is absolutely no doubt in my mind that this never would've happened were it not for the Five Essential Elements and for the support at HPC.'

Being the Real Deal

Recently, I was online, and an ad popped up for Masterclass, a well-known global e-learning platform that recruits key people of great influence to share their processes. This ad was for the famous comedian from back in the 80s and 90s, Steve Martin, and it started with him saying something like this: 'So many comedians come to me and they say, "Steve, I've got the agent and I've got the profile. I've got my Instagram set up. I've got my website. I've pretty much got everything I need. How can I be successful?" and I look at them and I say, "Don't you think you should focus on being funny?"'

His words struck a chord. I speak to so many coaches and they're telling me, 'Ryan, I've got my website, I've got my business cards. I've got my logos. I've got my accreditation. How do I create high-paying clients? How do I build this business?' And I say to them, 'What about focusing on coaching people?'

The magic ingredient of building your coaching business isn't the funnels, the landing pages, the podcasts, or the website. It's not your fluffy logos, your branding, your name, or your cool slogan. The secret to creating high-paying clients is your ability to help people have breakthroughs.

We built HPC off the back of one major thing: powerful coaching. It was the power of my coaching that made people want to work with me and us.

I've delivered, and never will stop delivering, powerful coaching. I coach people powerfully, and they share about that experience, their results, and our business. I coach people powerfully, which enables them to coach their clients powerfully too.

How could I give so many clients so many breakthroughs? Simple. I had these breakthroughs for myself first. Not just once but a million times over. It never ends. I see every breakdown as the next breakthrough. I'm committed to breaking through whatever stands in my way.

And I have learned to do that in a multitude of ways, from putting all my smallness on the table for all to see, holding my hand up to where I'm at (this is confronting!) to one day being able to sit in silence with all my fear and anxiety and learning how to simply be with it until it disappears. This was the most confronting challenge of all my challenges.

And with my clients? A commitment to being straight and great with them.

Let's get clear about what this is all about. If you want to build this business, you have to focus on your personal and professional breakthroughs, and with all that insight, you are left powerfully equipped to help your clients create breakthroughs too. From taking on and breaking through the idea that you might not be good enough to facing your fear of failure, it doesn't matter. It's all just the next breakthrough, and if you take it on like that, you will begin to show up for yourself and other people in a way that's utterly unimaginable to you right now. With those insights and new skills, you will create more results. You'll be more powerful in your coaching, and your clients will start creating more results, and on and on it goes.

You are High-Vibrational, and I call this being the Real Deal. If you want to build a deeply impactful and highly successful coaching business that makes an impact and leaves a mark on people's lives, then you've got to be committed to being the Real Deal. Whatever you are empowering your clients to lean into and break through is something you have already leaned into and broken through over and over.

If you're asking your clients to take the risk and spend the money, you've got to be taking the risks and spending the money.

Believe your clients can benefit from having a coach or being part of a program? Have a coach or be part of a program!

Asking your clients to let something go? Let it all go.

Inviting them to believe they can be, do, and have what they want? Be willing to believe it too and go be, do, and have it!

Show your clients the way

If you want to be the Real Deal, you've got to be doing everything you're asking your clients to do, but not just once or twice, or at the start or in the middle, or when you feel like it — but as a way of life. This is not about being perfect or having to get it right; being the Real Deal is also about embracing our humanity and being OK with things the way they are versus resisting them. Being the Real Deal is about learning how to be present, peaceful, calm, grounded, centred, kind, generous, caring, empowered, perfect in your imperfection, trusting, patient, compassionate, graceful, authentic, responsible, having integrity, unstoppable, unshakeable, being an example to yourself and your clients, and doing all that while keeping a great sense of humour and having fun! Being in love with yourself and all your human frailty. What an opportunity! Take yourself on like that, and incredible things will start to happen.

You can have anything you want to create for yourself, your life, or your business. It can be done, and you can do it. You've just got to allow yourself to see any limitation standing in your way as the next breakthrough — and break through it. It will take a relentless kind of commitment and courage to face yourself and anything that gets in your way. Hold yourself to the idea of being the Real Deal for yourself, your clients, and in the presence of your friends, partner, family, and in your life, as much as possible.

Do this and you'll not only be successful; you will be free. You will create all the impact you deeply want to make in the world. When you go to bed at night, you will do so with complete peace of mind. When you wake up in the morning, you will do so with energy and a sense of fulfilment money can't buy. You'll even start to look and be more attractive because of your shift in energy.

Whether you're still struggling to believe all this is possible for you or not is OK. Sit with this idea, contemplate it, and let it go to work on you.

This is a process, and it takes time. Trust it.

Consider that it all starts with a willingness to believe

From that space, you will find openings to take action, the most powerful and effective of which have all been laid out for you in this book.

Each and every action, each and every invitation, each and every resource, opening, opportunity, and idea laid out in this book will, if you take it on, lead you, step by step, bit by bit, to becoming a world-class High-Performing Coach.

Final Word

Here's my last question for you: How much do you love coaching, on a scale of 1–10? That is to say, how much do you love making a difference to people through the power of your coaching? What's your number, 1–10?

If you've read this far, I'm gonna bet your number was somewhere between 10 and 10,000,000.

Mine too!

The road to becoming a High-Performing Coach and building a thriving business is no easy feat. It's one challenge after the next — you'll have to really face yourself and push through all your limits; you'll have to grow way beyond who you are right now into who you'll become. You have to develop Unshakeable Belief, your Business Foundations, the Breakthrough Process, your online authority, and to break into a top and high-value Accountability & Coaching structure. It's a metamorphosis — scary, confronting, and painful at times! There's a lot to figure out and deal with, make no mistake about it.

The one thing that's going to empower you through the journey is this: your love of coaching.

You absolutely love coaching people.

You are energised to give away all you have learned.

It's an honour, and it's humbling, rewarding, fulfilling, exciting, and fun!

So, in the midst of your challenges, don't forget this. Don't forget to express it, don't forget to be grateful for what you're able to do each and every day, and coach as much as you possibly can — because it's your love of coaching that's going to fuel your fire and keep you going, no matter what.

Go light up the world with your love for coaching, with your love for making a difference and showing people how life can look when you're that lit up about who you get to be and what you get to do.

Coach as many people as you can just for the absolute love of it, and if you do that? Well, that's how I built an online, high-fee coaching business from the heart, and that's how you can do the same.

I wish you courage on your journey and that you may tread this path grounded, determined, enjoying the process of your evolution, nourished by the difference you get to make, believing that it can be done and you can do it!

Thank you for letting me into your world, thank you for your partnership, and most of all, thank you for who you are.

Love,
Ryan

What's Next?

If you'd like to explore how we could work together send me an email and tell me about what you got from reading this book and ask me about my group programs and opportunities to work privately together.

ryan@ryanmathie.com

Visit my website, www.ryanmathie.com

Follow me on LinkedIn linkedin.com/in/ryanmathie

Good luck with whatever you are creating, I look forward to hearing from you!

More Client Stories

Maureen is a career coach based in Hutto, Texas, U.S., who is passionate about helping people find or transition to their dream job.

Maureen had not done direct career coaching at all prior to committing to working with us. She was doing resume writing and job interview coaching, losing interest and focus, and making very little return for the amount of effort she put in. She had become dissatisfied, which kept her from being her usual 'positive self'. She was ready to give up.

When we started a conversation with Maureen, she had an epiphany and realised she wanted to become a career coach. 'As soon as I saw the word "coach", and the idea went in my head, I knew that is what I wanted to do going forward. It was a blazing moment of realisation, and I never looked back!' she said.

For Maureen, one of biggest impacts of working with us was that she discovered the joy of coaching people to break through blocks and work to reach their full potential. This has given her more joy than any executive position she held previously. 'In HPC, I have seen master coaches at work and applied their principles to my coaching. I am inspired to keep learning and grow my business.

'I jumped in with both feet despite having no formal career coaching training. However, my entire previous career of executive leadership, recruiting, resume writing, career counselling, and job interview coaching had helped prepare me for this moment. I struggled to create a career coaching program, but I followed the ideas presented in the training to develop my niche, and I have now successfully coached people. Emphasising serving, and not worrying about any other agenda, has given me freedom to share as much of my knowledge as is useful to the client.'

Maureen's life has been a hard struggle due to a very severe physical disability that's meant she has spent most of it in a wheelchair. During this time, she has learned to persevere, overcome adversity, and achieve success. 'My parents gave me an Unshakeable Belief in myself, and that has been reinforced by my ability to achieve my goals through persistence and hard work. HPC taught me that this Unshakeable Belief is an important competitive advantage, and I have been able to use that to enrol people so that I can help them with their career. I can show them how to have an Unshakeable Belief in themselves.'

Maureen created her career coaching program by following the strategies we outlined for her. 'It took a lot of work on my part to synthesize my previous experience into a coherent program (which I constantly tweak). Prior to the HPC course, I had never done career coaching, so I was starting from the ground up. To date, I have made as much revenue in four months as I made in a year in my previous job.'

Maureen learned how valuable her skills and insights were and now is not afraid to charge a fee for her work that is high, reasonable, and a match for the value that she brings.

Online, she was astounded by the success that her posts have had in creating useful advice and increasing her connections. 'I feel greatly enriched by my experience at HPC. I have seen personal growth and have applied the coaching techniques I have seen in action to my personal and business life. I have been an entrepreneur for several decades, and this whole experience has been so fulfilling I plan to continue with my own business.'

Mark is an England-based coach who supports people in business to overcome mental health crises such as depression, trauma, and burnout so they can go on to achieve their personal and professional ambitions and dreams.

'Prior to working with HPC, I had been running my coaching and therapy business for five years. By some measurements, I was successful. I started with zero clients in August 2015, and by March 2020, I was regularly seeing between 15 and 20 clients a week. Looking back, I was burning out. I was only charging £60 per session, so while I had a good client base, I was needing to work six and a half days a week to make only a small profit once my fixed costs were taken into account. And all of the additional activities of running a business, such as social media, had to be done on top of my client work. I had many plans for my business, but they just gathered dust on a metaphorical drawing board.'

Mark charged £60 per session because he absolutely believed he could not charge any more, and because, prior to working with HPC, he had not even heard of the idea of value-based fees. 'I let my local marketplace determine my value and my fees. I can remember as clear as day my first free HPC workshop and laughing out loud at some of the figures being bandied about by other attendees: £3K, £5K, even £10K. I thought Ryan was crazy! Once the HPC penny dropped, once I realised that so much of my own significant stress was due to the fact that I was not charging based on the value I was delivering for my clients, things started to change. I now charge what I am worth, which has not only improved my mental health and well-being, but also given me the time to take my ideas off the drawing board and make them a reality.'

With regards to his enrolment calls, Mark used to find it hard telling new or prospective clients that he charged £60, whereas now he tells them with complete confidence what his higher fees are. 'The connect-to-breakthrough strategy, combined with my own breakthroughs, have transformed an impossible business fantasy into a reality.

'Before, I was absolutely a product of my environment. It was limited and so was I. It was small and so was I. HPC has connected me to parts of the coaching industry I never even knew existed.

'I am confident and ambitious, while being grounded and realistic. Building a successful coaching business is hard work, and HPC is honest and transparent about this. However, the facts do not lie. In the first three months, I have made just shy of £12K. I am a better, more confident coach and am happy to call myself a businessman who also coaches, not just a coach who has a website.'

Jenn wanted to build her business as an enneagram coach and help leaders and teams communicate better based on personality assessments. Past training blindly told her to just say she was an enneagram coach and that people will 'flock to you'. That was not her experience.

'I really had no idea how to run a coaching business,' Jenn says.

'I was a speaker and writer who got a coaching certification because I wanted to help more people. I had a website, lots of content, but no clients. I had made $1,000 total from my speaking and about $400 from coaching. I had no idea how to change the trajectory of my business.'

Before working with HPC, Jenn was charging by the hour and struggling on her enrolment calls. To break through, she would need to shift into a high-fee model and learn how to create and enrol high-fee clients.

For Jenn, the Breakthrough Process created a profound change in her business and belief. 'I was throwing spaghetti against the wall before. But a process to follow gave me so much confidence ... I had shakeable thoughts before HPC. I didn't even realise how much I didn't believe in my abilities and how much my fear impacted my business.'

Unshakeable Belief changed Jenn's foundation.

The shift to a high-fee program changed her business entirely, and her ability to have powerful breakthrough conversations saw her clients become better served, as her business thrived and became sustainable. 'I created more than $40,000 in income from coaching and speaking in five months from starting with HPC, and now each and every month is five figures reliably ... I now know this can be a business that sustains my family and feeds my soul while I help people.'

Eighteen months after working with us, she became a TEDx Speaker.

Jenn helps teams and leaders solve conflict by improving communication and building self-awareness with the enneagram, so they can connect and create more powerful work.

Mary Ann is a Glasgow-based Business Success & Executive Coach. She helps entrepreneurs, business owners, and executives to be who they were made to be and build profitable businesses that create freedom and impact.

'I was already CEO of a couple of companies, so I understood business. I had been coaching for over 25 years and had decided to incorporate my coaching business as a separate entity so I could develop it with fresh eyes that were more aligned with the true me. I had clients, but they were in a niche that didn't bring me joy anymore.'

Mary Ann was in a place of exploration and transition when we met. She had just set up her coaching company as a separate entity from her other businesses. From launching and growing those other businesses, she understood the value of working with mentors and coaches in the same industry when in the initial stages of business building. 'The philosophy of HPC felt like it aligned with how I wanted to develop in my own business whilst bringing new ideas to the table. I was aware that due to the sheer scale of the coaching industry, being able to stand out in it as an independent coach was going to be potentially challenging without mentorship!

'"No conversations, no business" is a phrase of Ryan's I can hear in my head! HPC definitely made me much more aware of the need to TAKE ACTION to connect and market myself, not just more frequently but more CONSISTENTLY. This doubled up in value by being supported to put my best thinking out there in any moment — after 25 years of coaching, being "Messy vs. Right" wasn't easy but was critical to learning and building a business in a social and digital world! The support and encouragement of the HPC team was fundamental.'

Mary Ann had a lot of happy coaching clients in her many years' experience as a coach, but through HPC, she discovered within herself a completely new level of potential and value. 'I realised that although I had brought value to others in the past, I was limited as to how much impact I could have working with them if I didn't have an "Unshakeable Belief" in me. If that belief were missing, it would adversely impact every conversation I had and hinder the growth and impact of my business, as I would not always push forward into new and challenging opportunities that came my way! The self-value I now have allows such powerful conversations to happen, and the satisfaction I have in my life and business can sometimes feel positively overwhelming! Not to mention the extraordinary people I now meet and work with ... quite incredible!'

Mary Ann now has a waiting list for people wanting to work one-to-one with her as well as a high-fee group coaching program and a podcast about to launch! 'That isn't even everything that is going on — just the tip of the iceberg!! The opportunity ahead is now the only overwhelming thing in my life, which really isn't a bad place to be. HPC's support allowed me to understand what strategies were there for me to consider and how to implement them, but best of all, to understand that just being who I was made to be was enough to attract clients into my world, clients who would connect in the deepest and most meaningful way.'

The Breakthrough Process brought a framework to her coaching that supported her own growth and development. 'The way I had greater confidence to reach out to connect and invite people into my coaching space was transformative.

The framework enabled me to "up" the clarity and direction I was able to bring into their lives and to improve their ability to make confident and informed decisions about how to move forward. This transformation was sometimes mind-blowing! The satisfaction I now had in my work was off the scale and something I could never have imagined.'

'Night and day' is the expression Mary Ann uses to describe the impact HPC had on her online presence, and she knows that there is so much yet to come. 'They helped me to see that being online is a "practice". There is no end and perfect point. Each day brings new learning and new demands, and you need to be able to groove with it and have the systems and people in place to support you to do it well.

'I had a plan to build a six-figure coaching business, and I achieved that within the first ten months working in partnership with HPC. I say "partnership" because they consistently showed up, sharing everything they had in the most impactful way possible, but I had to show up that way too for it to create results, and it did! I have always loved coaching, but now I have more impact than ever before, which has brought a new level of joy to life and business that just keeps growing!'

About the Author

Ryan Mathie is a Scottish author, coach, and global award-winning expert in personal and professional development, best known as the co-founder of High-Performing Coach, a company that led as CEO since its inception in 2019 **until end of 2023**.

He was born in the small town of Bellshill in North Lanarkshire, Scotland, and is the great-nephew of the legendary Sir Matt Busby, CBE, KCSG, who was a Scottish football player and manager of the world-famous English football team Manchester United, achieving world-renowned success during his lengthy tenure at the club between 1945 and 1969.

At age twenty, Ryan moved to London, where he lived for eighteen years, with a short spell in the U.S. before he moved to the natural paradise of Madeira, Portugal, with his loving partner Jasmin, and they're little Pomeranian called Peach.

Ryan's personal and professional mastery developed since 2009 after a profound transformative experience while walking through the streets of Bethnal Green, London, which changed his life, leaving him with a desire to go even deeper and give away all that he had learned.

With more than 20,000 hours of coaching/development experience, Ryan is a leading figure amongst the rise of new coaches in the industry and is regarded by his clients and peers as one of the best, most highly trained, and effective coaches in the world.

As well as his passion for helping people living conscious and limitless lives, Ryan loves dogs, playing golf, wearing flip flops 'n' socks, solar gazing, meditating, plant-based food and being on time.

IT ALL STARTS WITH A
WILLINGNESS TO BELIEVE.

—RYAN MATHIE

Printed in Great Britain
by Amazon

47554574R00145